Quick Reference Guide

M000086543

Strategies

Page	Strategy	Focus		Text		When			Why									How			
		Comprehension	Vocabulary	Narrative	Informational	Before Reading	During Reading	After Reading	Predicting	Connecting	Questioning	Using Text Structure	Visualizing	Inferring	Summarizing	Synthesizing	Determining Importance	Individual	Partner	Small Group	Whole Group
77	Plus, Minus, Interesting	●		●	●			●		●				●				●	●	●	●
81	Possible Sentences	●	●		●	●	●	●	●	●				●				●	●		●
85	Predict-O-Gram	●	●	●		●	●	●	●		●	●		●				●	●	●	●
90	Prediction Chart	●		●	●	●	●		●	●								●	●	●	●
94	Questioning the Author	●		●	●		●			●					●	●		●	●	●	●
98	RIVET		●	●	●	●			●												●
102	Semantic Feature Analysis		●	●	●	●		●	●	●	●					●					●
106	Semantic Mapping	●	●	●	●	●	●	●		●						●	●	●		●	
110	Sketch to Stretch	●		●	●			●		●			●	●					●	●	●
113	Story Face	●		●				●					●	●			●	●		●	●
117	Story Pyramid	●		●				●		●					●	●		●	●	●	●
121	Strategy Glove	●		●	●		●	●				●	●				●	●	●	●	●
126	Tiered Bingo	●	●	●	●	●	●	●	●	●	●	●	●	●	●	●	●	●			
131	Vocabulary Anchors		●		●	●				●	●									●	●
136	Word Sorts	●			●			●	●				●					●	●	●	●

Comprehension and Vocabulary Strategies for the Primary Grades

Evidence-Based Strategies

Jerry L. Johns

Susan Davis Lenski

Roberta L. Berglund

Reproducible Masters

Quick Reference Guide

KENDALL/HUNT PUBLISHING COMPANY

4050 Westmark Drive Dubuque, Iowa 52002

www.kendallhunt.com

Book Team

Chairman and Chief Executive Officer   Mark C. Falb
Vice President, Director of National Book Program   Alfred C. Grisanti
Senior Vice President, College Division   Thomas W. Gantz
Editorial Developmental Manager   Georgia Botsford
Prepress Project Coordinator   Sheri Hosek
Prepress Editor   Ellen Kaune
Permissions Editor   Colleen Zelinsky
Design Manager   Jodi Splinter
Designer   Deb Howes

Ordering Information

Address: Kendall/Hunt Publishing Company
4050 Westmark Drive
Dubuque, IA 52004
Telephone: 800-247-3458, ext. 4 or 5
Web site: www.kendallhunt.com
Fax: 800-772-9165

Author Addresses for Correspondence and Workshops

Jerry L. Johns
Consultant in Reading
2105 Eastgate Drive
Sycamore, IL 60178
E-mail: *jjohns@niu.edu*
815-895-3022

Susan Davis Lenski
Illinois State University
Campus Box 5330
Normal, IL 61790-5330
E-mail: *sjlensk@ilstu.edu*
309-438-3028

Roberta L. Berglund
Consultant in Reading/Language Arts
Two Oak Brook Club Drive
Suite C-102
Oak Brook, IL 60523
E-mail: *bberglund@rocketmail.com*
630-782-5852

Only the resource pages with the Kendall/Hunt copyright footnote may be reproduced for noncommercial educational purposes without obtaining written permission from the publisher. This license is limited to you, the individual purchaser, for use with your own clients or students. It does not extend to additional professionals in your institution, school district, or other setting, nor does purchase by an institution constitute a site license. This license does not grant the right to reproduce these materials for resale, redistribution, or any other purposes (including but not limited to books, pamphlets, articles, videotapes or audiotapes, and handouts or slides for lectures or workshops). Permission to reproduce these materials for the above purposes or any other purpose must be obtained in writing from the Permissions Department of Kendall/Hunt Publishing Company.

Copyright © 2003 by Kendall/Hunt Publishing Company

ISBN 0-7872-9881-6

All rights reserved. No part of this publication may be reproduced, stored in a retrieval system, or transmitted, in any form or by any means, electronic, mechanical, photocopying, recording, or otherwise, without the prior written permission of the copyright owner.

Printed in the United States of America
10 9 8 7 6 5 4 3 2

 # PREFACE AND OVERVIEW

Who Will Use This Book?

We have written this practical and useful book for inservice and preservice teachers. The book is ideal for professional development in schools, districts, and other types of programs where the focus is on reading in the primary grades. It will also be a helpful supplement in undergraduate and graduate reading and language arts classes, as well as in clinical courses where there is a desire to provide useful strategies that have wide applicability with narrative and informational text.

What Are Some of the Outstanding Qualities of This Book?

There are several outstanding qualities of this book.

1. The book contains strategies that have utility in reading, as well as other areas of the curriculum.

2. The strategies are organized around two important areas: comprehension and vocabulary.

3. The strategies are presented with a unique and helpful chart that quickly shows when, why, and how to use them. The chart also indicates whether the strategy can be used with narrative text, informational text, or both.

4. The strategies are presented in an easy-to-follow, step-by-step manner.

5. Most of the strategies contain one or more examples.

6. A reproducible master accompanies each strategy.

What Grade Levels Do the Strategies Address?

The strategies in this book were specifically written for use in primary grades. After reading about a strategy, it should be quite easy for you to determine how best to use it with your students. You will probably want to adapt some of the strategies to fit your teaching style and your students' particular needs. For beginning readers, the strategies may be used with materials you read to students. You can then complete the strategy through shared reading and writing.

What Insights Have Been Provided by Research?

There is little doubt that teaching results in student learning. A persistent problem is that of teachers mentioning a skill or assigning a task without taking the time to teach it. Instruction that is characterized by clear explanation, modeling, and guided practice can increase student learning (Duffy, 2002). The National Reading Panel (2000) compiled a large volume that offers several strategies for effective comprehension instruction. According to Cunningham (2001), the comprehension section of the report is potentially valuable. Other major reviews (Pearson & Fielding, 1991; Tierney & Cunningham, 1984) and related writings (Ogle & Blachowicz, 2002; Pressley, 2000, 2002; Rand Study Group, 2002) support the following areas for an instructional focus.

1. Teach students to be aware of their own comprehension. This strategy is often referred to as comprehension monitoring.

2. Have students work together on their strategies. This strategy is called cooperative learning.

3. Have students make graphic summaries of what is read through the use of graphic and semantic organizers.

4. Use story [and text] structure.

5. Help students learn to ask and answer questions.

6. Teach students to summarize what is read.

Vocabulary knowledge plays a crucial, but complex, role in reading comprehension. The educational community has known for decades that vocabulary knowledge can strongly influence reading comprehension (Davis, 1944; Nagy & Scott, 2000). Research has shown that a relationship between vocabulary and comprehension exists (McKeown, Beck, Omanson, & Perfetti, 1983; McKeown, Beck, Omanson, & Pople, 1985; Tomeson & Aarnouste, 1998), and vocabulary instruction can play at least a partial role in that relationship (NRP, 2000). However, research also indicates that vocabulary instruction should provide students with a variety of rich experiences with words (Stahl & Fairbanks, 1986). Unfortunately, classroom instruction on vocabulary knowledge tends to be traditional, such as providing students with lists of words to look up in a dictionary (Blachowicz & Fisher, 2000, 2001). This simplistic reaction to the complexity of learning words, particularly as it relates to texts with vocabulary density, can hinder students from developing a rich comprehension of text. Vocabulary instruction embedded within authentic strategy instruction, therefore, has the potential for building vocabulary awareness, vocabulary knowledge, and a better comprehension of text.

The strategies selected for this book will help you in the areas of comprehension and vocabulary. The key ingredients, however, are your actions as the teacher.

• Take time to teach the strategies.

• Tell students how the strategies will help them become better readers.

• Model how the strategies are used.

• Think aloud by describing what goes on in your mind as you are using the strategy.

- Provide guided practice so students can learn how the strategy will help them understand the lesson or text.

- Reinforce students' efforts.

- Develop the strategies over time and remind students to use the strategies in a variety of contexts.

- Help students reflect on the strategies and how they help in particular contexts.

Finally, we want to stress again the critical importance of teaching the strategies. Many of the strategies can be embedded in oral reading you share with students. This means you can teach the strategies as students are in the process of becoming independent readers.

Is This Book Easy to Use?

Yes! The format and organization of this book makes it very user friendly. We have also included a Quick Reference Guide inside the front cover so you can quickly locate the various strategies and consider their use. Note that the strategies are listed in alphabetical order.

Where Should I Begin?

Glance at the Quick Reference Guide inside the front cover and on the first page. Scan the strategies and find a particular strategy that interests you. Turn to the page for that strategy. Suppose you select Character Four Square on page 20. Under the title, you will see a chart that covers five areas.

CHARACTER FOUR SQUARE

FOCUS		TEXT		WHEN			WHY									HOW			
Comprehension	Vocabulary	Narrative	Informational	Before Reading	During Reading	After Reading	Predicting	Connecting	Questioning	Using Text Structure	Visualizing	Inferring	Summarizing	Synthesizing	Determining Importance	Individual	Partner	Small Group	Whole Group
●	●	●				●		●			●					●	●	●	●

1. **FOCUS** indicates which areas (i.e., comprehension and vocabulary) are covered by the strategy. The dots indicate that Character Four Square focuses on comprehension and vocabulary.

2. **TEXT** refers to the type of text materials with which the strategies can be used. Narrative text refers to stories; informational text generally refers to nonfiction materials. The dot indicates Character Four Square would be best used with narrative materials.

3. **WHEN** tells you if you should use the strategy before, during, and/or after reading. The dot signifies that Character Four Square is best used after reading.

4. **WHY** is based on the work of Duke and Pearson (2002), Keene and Zimmermann (1997), Pearson, Roehler, Dole, and Duffy (1992) and others who have reviewed the research in comprehension. These areas help students become thoughtful, independent readers who are engaged in their reading and learning. Following are brief descriptions of the nine areas we use in this book.

   - *Predicting*—Students can make predictions about the content of a text from the title, illustrations, and headings. Students can also use their prior knowledge to anticipate word meanings or how words might be related.

   - *Connecting*—Students increase their comprehension when they think about how their lives are connected to the text and to the world.

   - *Questioning*—Asking questions engages students in an internal dialogue to clarify understanding. Questions can also be asked by teachers and other students.

   - *Using Text Structure*—Narrative and informational texts are organized differently. Students can use their knowledge of text structure to help understand and remember what the author wrote.

   - *Visualizing*—Students can create visual images based on words from the text. These images may be shared through discussions, sketches, or drawings.

   - *Inferring*—Students use what is known, as well as clues from the text, to contemplate and hypothesize about what was read.

   - *Summarizing*—Students can summarize while they read and after they read to better understand the author's message.

   - *Synthesizing*—Students use new information and their prior knowledge to create thoughts or perspectives.

   - *Determining Importance*—Students learn to identify the important ideas in printed materials and separate them from ideas that are less important.

   Character Four Square gives students an opportunity to use the processes of connecting and visualizing.

5. **HOW** refers to whether the strategy is best used with individuals, partners, small groups, and/or whole groups. Character Four Square can be used with individuals, partners, small groups, and whole groups.

Below the chart are the words *Description* and *Procedure*. There is a brief description of Character Four Square followed by a step-by-step procedure for using it. We like to think of the numbered steps as a systematic lesson plan to help you present the strategy to your students. You should, of course, feel free to adapt the steps and examples to fit your class.

Description

Character Four Square is a strategy to help teach or review characterization in a story. Students may make inferences to come up with some of the information requested. The information is then placed in four squares.

Procedure

1. Choose a book or story with a character (person or animal) that will be relatively easy for students to describe. Initially, use a short text with one main character to read to the entire class.

2. Make an overhead transparency of the reproducible master on page 23 or draw a square with four quadrants on the board. Label them as shown in the example below. For younger students, you may wish to use the reproducible master on page 24.

Name	Physical Description
Feelings	Character Traits

We often provide one or more *examples* (see example below) of how the strategy might be used in your curriculum. You may quickly be able to think of logical extensions to your lessons in a variety of areas.

Character Four Square
The Bird, the Frog, and the Light by Avi

Name	Physical Description
Frog	yellow toes big green bulging wore a crown
Feelings important sad	**Character Traits** bossy proud mean impatient

To make the strategy especially useful, a *reproducible master* is included. You have the publisher's permission to reproduce and use the master with your students within the guidelines noted on the copyright page of this book.

References

Blachowicz, C.L.Z., & Fisher, P. (2000). Vocabulary instruction. In M.L. Kamil, P.B. Mosenthal, P.D. Pearson, & R. Barr (Eds.), *Handbook of reading research* (Vol. III) (pp. 503–523). Mahwah, NJ: Erlbaum.

Blachowicz, C., & Fisher, P. (2001). *Teaching vocabulary in all classrooms* (2nd ed.). Upper Saddle River, NJ: Merrill Prentice Hall.

Cunningham, J.W. (2001). The National Reading Panel Report (Essay Book Review). *Reading Research Quarterly*, *36*, 326–335.

Davis, F.B. (1944). Fundamental factors in reading comprehension. *Psychometrika*, *9*, 185–197.

Duffy, G.G. (2002). The case for direct explanation of strategies. In C.C. Block & M. Pressley (Eds.), *Comprehension instruction: Research-based best practices* (pp. 28–41). New York: Guilford.

Duke, N.K., & Pearson, P.D. (2002). Effective practices for developing reading comprehension. In A.E. Farstrup & S.J. Samuels (Eds.), *What research has to say about reading instruction* (3rd ed.) (pp. 205–242). Newark, DE: International Reading Association.

Keene, E.O., & Zimmermann, S. (1997). *Mosaic of thought*. Portsmouth, NH: Heinemann.

McKeown, M.G., Beck, I.L., Omanson, R.C., & Perfetti, C.A. (1983). The effects of long-term vocabulary instruction on reading comprehension: A replication. *Journal of Reading Behavior*, *15*, 3–18.

McKeown, M.G., Beck, I.L., Omanson, R.C., & Pople, M.T. (1985). Some effects of the nature and frequency of vocabulary instruction on the knowledge and use of words. *Reading Research Quarterly, 20,* 522–535.

Nagy, W.E., & Scott, J.A. (2000). Vocabulary processes. In M.L. Kamil, P.B. Mosenthal, P.D. Pearson, & R. Barr (Eds.), *Handbook of reading research* (Vol. III) (pp. 269–284). Mahwah, NJ: Erlbaum.

National Reading Panel. (2000). *Teaching children to read: An evidence-based assessment of the scientific research literature on reading and its implications for reading instruction.* Washington, DC: National Institute for Child Health & Human Development.

Ogle, D., & Blachowicz, C.L.Z. (2002). Beyond literature circles: Helping students comprehend informational text. In C.C. Block & M. Pressley (Eds.), *Comprehension instruction: Research-based best practices* (pp. 259–274). New York: Guilford.

Pearson, P.D., & Fielding, L. (1991). Comprehension instruction. In R. Barr, M.L. Kamil, P.B. Mosenthal, & P.D. Pearson (Eds.), *Handbook of reading research* (Vol. II) (pp. 815–816). White Plains, NY: Longman.

Pearson, P.D., Roehler, L.R., Dole, J.A., & Duffy, G.G. (1992). Developing expertise in reading comprehension. In S.J. Samuels & A.E. Farstrup (Eds.) *What research has to say about reading instruction* (2nd ed.) (pp. 153–169). Newark, DE: International Reading Association.

Pressley, M. (2000). What should comprehension instruction be the instruction of? In M.L. Kamil, P.B. Mosenthal, P.D. Pearson, & R. Barr (Eds.), *Handbook of reading research* (Vol. III) (pp. 545–561). Mahwah, NJ: Erlbaum.

Pressley, M. (2002). Comprehension strategies instruction: A turn-of-the-century status report. In C.C. Block & M. Pressley (Eds.), *Comprehension instruction: Research-based best practices* (pp. 11–27). New York: Guilford.

Rand Study Group. (2002). *Reading for understanding: Toward an R&D program in reading comprehension.* Santa Monica, CA: Author.

Stahl, S., & Fairbanks, M. (1986). The effects of vocabulary instruction: A model-based meta-analysis. *Review of Educational Research, 56,* 72–110.

Tierney, R.J., & Cunningham, J.W. (1984). Research on teaching reading comprehension. In P.D. Pearson, R. Barr, M.L. Kamil, & P. Mosenthal (Eds.), *Handbook of reading research* (Vol. I) (pp. 609–655). White Plains, NY: Longman.

Tomesen, M., & Aarnouste, C. (1998). Effects of an instructional programme for deriving word meanings. *Educational Studies, 24,* 107–128.

ACKNOWLEDGMENTS

We are grateful to the many professionals whose research and writing provided a basis for this book. There were also teachers and students whose insights were extremely helpful. Rita Shafer and students at Pleasant Lane Elementary School (District 44) in Lombard, Illinois, provided helpful and practical advice. Three teachers at the Thomwell School for the Arts in Hartsville, South Carolina, graciously read and reacted to many of the strategies: Meredith Askins, Naomi Player, and Maria A. Williams. Dawn Andermann, a reading teacher, prepared the initial drafts of several strategies. All of these teachers and students helped us prepare a better book. Special thanks to Annette Johns, Mary C. Leahy, Bethany Phillips, and Joan Will for reading the final manuscript for accuracy and clarity.

Jerry, Sue, and Bobbi

Jerry L. Johns, Distinguished Teaching Professor Emeritus of Northern Illinois University, is the 2002–2003 president of the International Reading Association. He has been recognized as a distinguished professor, writer, and outstanding teacher educator. He has taught students from kindergarten through college and serves as a consultant and speaker to schools and professional organizations.

Dr. Johns is a past president of the Illinois Reading Council, College Reading Association, and Northern Illinois Reading Council. He has received recognition for outstanding service to each of these professional organizations and is a member of the Illinois Reading Council Hall of Fame. Dr. Johns has served on numerous committees of the International Reading Association and was a member of the Board of Directors. He has also received the Outstanding Teacher Educator in Reading Award from the International Reading Association and the Champion for Children Award from the HOSTS Corporation.

Dr. Johns has been invited to consult, conduct workshops, and make presentations for teachers and professional groups throughout the United States and Canada. He has also prepared nearly 300 publications that have been useful to a diverse group of educators. His *Basic Reading Inventory*, now in its eighth edition, is widely used in undergraduate and graduate classes, as well as by practicing teachers. Dr. Johns recently coauthored the third edition of *Improving Reading: Strategies and Resources* and the second edition of *Teaching Beginning Readers: Linking Assessment and Instruction*.

Susan Davis Lenski is an Associate Professor at Illinois State University, in the Department of Curriculum and Instruction, where she teaches undergraduate and graduate courses in reading, writing, language arts, and literacy theory. Dr. Lenski brings 20 years of experience as a public school teacher to her work as a professor, writer, and researcher. As a result of her practical experience and her grounding in theory, Dr. Lenski is a popular speaker for professional development programs and has consulted in the United States, Canada, and Guatemala.

Dr. Lenski has been recognized for her work by a variety of organizations. For her work in schools as a teacher, she received the Nila Banton Smith Award and led her school to receive an Exemplary Reading Program Award, both from the International Reading Association. In Illinois, Dr. Lenski was inducted into the Illinois Reading Council Hall of Fame, and at Illinois State University, Dr. Lenski was named Outstanding Researcher.

AUTHORS

Dr. Lenski has co-authored eight books, including *Improving Reading: Strategies and Resources,* and has published over 50 articles in state and national journals. Her research interests include intertextuality during reading and writing; incorporating strategies into classroom practice, and preparing culturally responsive teachers.

Roberta L. (Bobbi) Berglund has had a long and distinguished career in education. Her public school experience spans more than 20 years and includes serving as a classroom teacher, reading specialist, Title I Director, and district curriculum administrator. Dr. Berglund has been a member of the reading faculty at the University of Wisconsin-Whitewater and has also taught graduate reading courses at Northern Illinois University, Rockford College, National-Louis University, and Aurora University. Currently Dr. Berglund is a consultant in the area of reading and language arts, working with school districts and regional offices of education in developing curriculum and assessment, conducting staff development, and guiding the selection of instructional materials for reading, spelling, writing, and related areas.

Dr. Berglund has received honors for outstanding service to several organizations and has been selected as a member of the Illinois Reading Council Hall of Fame. She also was honored with the Those Who Excel Award from the Illinois State Board of Education.

Dr. Berglund has served on several committees of the International Reading Association, including the program committee for the World Congress in Scotland and as chair of the Publications Committee. She has worked extensively with an international team of reading professionals to develop an on-line electronic journal and, most recently, has participated in the development of an early literacy assessment.

Dr. Berglund has conducted numerous workshops for teachers and has been invited to make presentations at state, national, and international conferences. She is the author of over fifty publications and is the coauthor of three professional books, including *Fluency: Questions, Answers, and Evidence-Based Strategies.*

ANTICIPATION/ REACTION GUIDE

FOCUS		TEXT		WHEN			WHY									HOW			
Comprehension	Vocabulary	Narrative	Informational	Before Reading	During Reading	After Reading	Predicting	Connecting	Questioning	Using Text Structure	Visualizing	Inferring	Summarizing	Synthesizing	Determining Importance	Individual	Partner	Small Group	Whole Group
●		●	●	●	●	●	●	●	●			●		●		●	●	●	●

Description

Before students begin reading, they should activate their prior knowledge. A strategy that prompts students to think about the key concepts of a story or selection before they read is an Anticipation Guide (Herber, 1978). The key concepts can be facts that the students will learn from reading, or they can be opinion statements. An Anticipation Guide can also be used after reading to confirm or alter students' ideas and is commonly called a Reaction Guide. This strategy, therefore, can help students make predictions before reading, and it can also provide a framework for checking the accuracy of the predictions.

Procedure

1. Identify a selection, either fiction or nonfiction, which you want students to read. The story should contain facts that students could learn or key concepts from which students can develop opinions.

2. List the facts or the concepts that you want students to learn. For example, if you want students to read *Pigs* by Gibbons (1991), you might list the following terms and ideas.

   - piglet
   - not dirty
   - intelligent
   - grow fast
   - not always pink

3. After you have identified terms and ideas, create sentences that could be answered with a "yes" or a "no." Do not write open-ended questions. For example, you should write, "A baby pig is called a piglet," rather than asking, "What is a baby pig called?" Some Anticipation/Reaction Guide sentences appear below.

   - A baby pig is called a piglet.
   - Pigs are smelly and dirty animals.
   - Pigs are the smartest of all farm animals.

- Pigs grow faster than any other farm animal.
- All pigs are pink.

4. Duplicate a copy of the blank Anticipation/Reaction Guide Sheet on page 4. Write the sentences on the lines.

5. Duplicate and distribute copies of your completed Anticipation/Reaction Guide to students. Tell students that you want to know what they think *before* reading the book *Pigs*. Emphasize that you don't expect students to know the answers, but that you want them to make their best guesses about whether the statements are correct or incorrect.

6. Read one of the statements with students. For example, read the statement "A baby pig is called a piglet." Ask them to decide whether they think the answer is "yes" or "no." Tell students to circle the answer that they think is correct to the left of the statements. Encourage students to work independently.

7. Have students read the remaining statements or read them to the students. Tell students to respond to each statement with their best guess.

8. After students have finished, tell them to read or listen to the story, paying special attention to the ideas presented in the Anticipation/Reaction Guide statements.

9. After students have read the story, have them revisit the Anticipation/Reaction Guide by reacting to the statements once more. This time have students respond to the right of the statements. After reading, discuss the idea that readers can change their minds while reading by saying something like the following.

> When you read, you have some ideas before you begin, just like we did before we read the book *Pigs*. Most of us thought that pigs are smelly and dirty before we read the story, but we found out that pigs are really very clean animals. We learned something when we read this book, so we changed our minds about the statement, "Pigs are smelly and dirty animals." After we read, we need to think about what we have learned and whether we need to change our minds about something.

10. An Anticipation/Reaction Guide using opinion rather then factual statements can be found on page 3, and a reproducible master of an Anticipation/Reaction Guide is on page 4.

References

Herber, H.H. (1978). *Teaching reading in the content areas* (2nd ed.). Englewood Cliffs, NJ: Prentice-Hall.

Gibbons, G. (1991). *Pigs*. New York: Scholastic.

Wyeth, S.D. (1998). *Something beautiful*. New York: Random House.

Anticipation/Reaction Guide

Something Beautiful by S. D. Wyeth

DIRECTIONS Before reading or listening to the story *Something Beautiful*, decide whether you agree or disagree with each of these statements. Circle "yes" or "no." After reading, think about whether you still agree or disagree or whether you want to change your mind. Circle "yes" or "no."

Before Reading			After Reading	
(Yes)	No	1. Everyone should have something beautiful.	Yes	No
Yes	(No)	2. When life is hard, there's nothing you can do.	Yes	No
Yes	(No)	3. The same thing makes everyone happy.	Yes	No
(Yes)	No	4. People can find something beautiful if they try.	Yes	No

 # Anticipation/Reaction Guide

Title and Author

DIRECTIONS Before reading or listening, decide whether you agree or disagree with each of these statements. Circle "yes" or "no." After reading think about whether you still agree or disagree or whether you want to change your mind. Circle "yes" or "no."

Before Reading   After Reading

Yes No   1. _____   Yes No

                        _____.

Yes No   2. _____   Yes No

                        _____.

Yes No   3. _____   Yes No

                        _____.

Yes No   4. _____   Yes No

                        _____.

Yes No   5. _____   Yes No

                        _____.

Yes No   6. _____   Yes No

                        _____.

From Jerry L. Johns, Susan Davis Lenski, and Roberta L. Berglund, *Comprehension and Vocabulary Strategies for the Primary Grades*. Copyright © 2003 by Kendall/Hunt Publishing Company (1-800-247-3458, ext. 4 or 5). May be reproduced for noncommercial educational purposes within the guidelines noted on the copyright page.

BOOKMARK STRATEGY PROMPTS

FOCUS		TEXT		WHEN			WHY									HOW			
Comprehension	Vocabulary	Narrative	Informational	Before Reading	During Reading	After Reading	Predicting	Connecting	Questioning	Using Text Structure	Visualizing	Inferring	Summarizing	Synthesizing	Determining Importance	Individual	Partner	Small Group	Whole Group
•	•	•	•		•		•	•	•		•	•	•	•	•	•		•	•

Description

After strategies have been taught to students, there is a continuing need to give them opportunities to practice the strategies during reading. Some students may not remember the strategies or realize when a particular strategy may be useful. To help overcome these concerns, several different Bookmark Strategy Prompts are provided for your use.

Procedure

1. Review the different sets of Bookmark Strategy Prompts on pages 7 through 10 and duplicate the page that is most appropriate for your students. Or, you can create your own prompts. The bookmarks can be duplicated on card stock and laminated so they last longer.

2. Be sure that you have taught the various strategies on a particular bookmark or teach the Bookmark Strategy Prompts. You can focus on a single strategy initially and then add additional strategies in subsequent lessons. General guidelines for teaching each strategy are listed below.

    *   Create an awareness of the strategy. Help students understand how learning and using the strategy will make them better readers.
    *   Define or explain the strategy using terminology that students will understand.
    *   Model the strategy with instructional materials in your classroom. One way to model is to think aloud as you process the information.
    *   Provide students practice in the use of the strategy through the use of interesting and appropriate materials.
    *   Encourage students to use the strategy as they engage in a wide variety of reading situations. The Bookmark Strategy Prompts are very useful reminders of strategies that can be used.

3. Use the bookmark with the whole group, smaller groups who read at approximately the same level, or groups who may need to learn or practice a particular strategy. As you teach the strategy, you might say something like the following.

    Today in our group we are going to use our bookmark while we read. There are many ideas on the bookmark to help us know what to do when we read. We are going to focus on the idea titled "fix my mistakes." Take a crayon or marker and circle that item on your bookmark. [Take time to review what the phrase "fix my mistakes" means. See bookmark on page 8.]

4. Have students read the first page in the selected text silently. They should pay particular attention to any mistakes they make and what they do to fix them (or to try to fix them). After students have read the page, allow time for them to share their mistakes and the strategies they used to make sense of their reading. A sample interchange follows.

    Mrs. West: Let's share what we did to fix our mistakes.

    Cote: I first read *eat* [for *munch*] because the picture showed the children eating. It didn't make sense to say *eat on carrots,* so I went back and reread the sentence and came up with the word *munch*. It made sense and looked like the right word.

    David: I wasn't sure if I pronounced *Lin* correctly. I said it like Lynn in our room, but the words are spelled differently. I think I'm correct. Am I?

    Mrs. West: Yes, you are correct. It was very good that you were able to relate *Lin* to another word you knew.

5. Use a similar approach with other elements on the Bookmark Strategy Prompts. As students develop greater competence with the strategies, encourage their use during independent reading. From time to time, it is also a good idea to model the bookmark elements during instruction with small groups or the entire class.

What's the word?

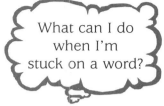

What can I do when I'm stuck on a word?

1. Look at the pictures.

2. Get your mouth ready for the beginning sound. *t-t-t*

3. Read on and come back to the word.

4. Put in a word that would make sense.

5. Look for the little parts that I know.
   CANDY
   C-AND-Y

6. Ask someone for help.

What's the word?

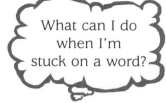

What can I do when I'm stuck on a word?

1. Look at the pictures.

2. Get your mouth ready for the beginning sound. *t-t-t*

3. Read on and come back to the word.

4. Put in a word that would make sense.

5. Look for the little parts that I know.
   CANDY
   C-AND-Y

6. Ask someone for help.

What's the word?

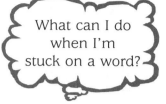

What can I do when I'm stuck on a word?

1. Look at the pictures.

2. Get your mouth ready for the beginning sound. *t-t-t*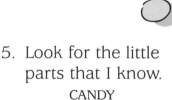

3. Read on and come back to the word.

4. Put in a word that would make sense.

5. Look for the little parts that I know.
   CANDY
   C-AND-Y

6. Ask someone for help.

From Jerry L. Johns, Susan Davis Lenski, and Roberta L. Berglund, *Comprehension and Vocabulary Strategies for the Primary Grades*. Copyright © 2003 by Kendall/Hunt Publishing Company (1-800-247-3458, ext. 4 or 5). May be reproduced for noncommercial educational purposes within the guidelines noted on the copyright page.

What can I do to understand what I read?

1. Make a prediction and check to see if I am right.

2. Try to make a picture in my head.

3. Look at pictures in the book.

4. Think about what is happening.

5. Look for words I know.

6. Look at word bits and parts.

7. Fix my mistakes.

8. Read ahead.

9. Read it again to myself.

10. Read it again aloud.

11. Remember what happened first, next, and last.

12. Tell in a sentence what it is about.

13. Think, "Does this make sense?"

What can I do to understand what I read?

1. Make a prediction and check to see if I am right.

2. Try to make a picture in my head.

3. Look at pictures in the book.

4. Think about what is happening.

5. Look for words I know.

6. Look at word bits and parts.

7. Fix my mistakes.

8. Read ahead.

9. Read it again to myself.

10. Read it again aloud.

11. Remember what happened first, next, and last.

12. Tell in a sentence what it is about.

13. Think, "Does this make sense?"

What can I do to understand what I read?

1. Make a prediction and check to see if I am right.

2. Try to make a picture in my head.

3. Look at pictures in the book.

4. Think about what is happening.

5. Look for words I know.

6. Look at word bits and parts.

7. Fix my mistakes.

8. Read ahead.

9. Read it again to myself.

10. Read it again aloud.

11. Remember what happened first, next, and last.

12. Tell in a sentence what it is about.

13. Think, "Does this make sense?"

From Jerry L. Johns, Susan Davis Lenski, and Roberta L. Berglund, *Comprehension and Vocabulary Strategies for the Primary Grades*. Copyright © 2003 by Kendall/Hunt Publishing Company (1-800-247-3458, ext. 4 or 5). May be reproduced for noncommercial educational purposes within the guidelines noted on the copyright page.

Reading Strategies I
Have Used

_____ Predicting

_____ Connecting

_____ Questioning

_____ Visualizing

_____ Inferring

_____ Determining
Importance

_____ Summarizing/
Synthesizing

Reading Strategies I
Have Used

_____ Predicting

_____ Connecting

_____ Questioning

_____ Visualizing

_____ Inferring

_____ Determining
Importance

_____ Summarizing/
Synthesizing

From Jerry L. Johns, Susan Davis Lenski, and Roberta L. Berglund, _Comprehension and Vocabulary Strategies for the Primary Grades_. Copyright © 2003 by Kendall/Hunt Publishing Company (1-800-247-3458, ext. 4 or 5). May be reproduced for noncommercial educational purposes within the guidelines noted on the copyright page.

GOOD READERS

Make Predictions
about what will be in the
text.

Make Connections
between the text, their lives,
the world, and other books.

Ask Questions
of the author, of
themselves, of the text.

**Make Pictures in
Their Minds**
as they read and
change them as they
get new information.

Make Inferences
Use what is known and
clues in the text to
make judgments or predict.

Determine Important Information
Figure out what ideas
are most important to
the meaning.

Synthesize
New information + what is known =
new idea or interpretation.

Use Fix Up Strategies
When they don't understand,
they read that part again,
read ahead, adjust reading
speed, or ask for help.

GOOD READERS

Make Predictions
about what will be in the
text.

Make Connections
between the text, their lives,
the world, and other books.

Ask Questions
of the author, of
themselves, of the text.

**Make Pictures in
Their Minds**
as they read and
change them as they
get new information.

Make Inferences
Use what is known and
clues in the text to
make judgments or predict.

Determine Important Information
Figure out what ideas
are most important to
the meaning.

Synthesize
New information + what is known =
new idea or interpretation.

Use Fix Up Strategies
When they don't understand,
they read that part again,
read ahead, adjust reading
speed, or ask for help.

From Jerry L. Johns, Susan Davis Lenski, and Roberta L. Berglund, *Comprehension and Vocabulary Strategies for the Primary Grades*. Copyright © 2003 by Kendall/Hunt Publishing Company (1-800-247-3458, ext. 4 or 5). May be reproduced for noncommercial educational purposes within the guidelines noted on the copyright page.

BRAIN SURFING

FOCUS		TEXT		WHEN			WHY									HOW			
Comprehension	Vocabulary	Narrative	Informational	Before Reading	During Reading	After Reading	Predicting	Connecting	Questioning	Using Text Structure	Visualizing	Inferring	Summarizing	Synthesizing	Determining Importance	Individual	Partner	Small Group	Whole Group
●	●	●			●	●		●	●				●	●		●	●	●	●

Description

Students' reading comprehension can be enriched when they discuss their interpretations of stories after reading. Strategies that help students make connections to their lives, to other texts, and to the subjects that they've been learning are especially valuable. One strategy that fosters connections after reading is Brain Surfing (Lenski, 2001). Brain Surfing encourages students to think about meanings after reading by "surfing" their brain like they would surf the Internet for material.

Procedure

1. Identify a book that you would like to read to your class or that you want your students to read silently. If students read the book silently, make sure the book is at a level that everyone can comprehend. Choose books that have the potential for connections to all subject areas that you teach.

2. Duplicate and distribute a reproducible master of the Brain Surfing graphic on page 15 or draw the graphic on the board.

3. Tell students that after you read the book you will be asking them to "surf their brains" and think about connections to the book. For example, you might say something like the following.

    > Today I'm going to read a book to you called *The Family of Earth* (Schimmel, 2001). While I'm reading and after I'm finished, I'd like you to "surf your brain" for connections. The connections you make could be to your own life, to other books you have read or to the other subjects that we've been learning in school: math, social studies, science, art, physical education, music, and language arts. I'd like you to think of "surfing your brain" like you surf the Internet. You move from one website to another, opening websites that interest you. Think of your brain as having different websites for each of the areas we discussed.

4. Draw students' attention to the Brain Surfing sheet. Identify each of the areas for which they could make a connection. Tell students something like the following.

    You can see on the graphic that we have circles of each of the areas where you'll be making connections. While I'm reading *The Family of Earth*, I'd like you to "surf your brains" and think of connections to each of these areas. If you make a connection, write it down in the circle so that you remember your connections for our class discussion after I finish reading.

5. Begin reading the book to students. Stop periodically and invite students to make connections.

6. After reading, provide students with a few more minutes to make connections and write them on the Brain Surfing sheet. Then discuss the connections students have made. A sample class discussion follows.

    Mrs. Kinzinger: What connections did you make to *The Family of Earth*?

    Tamika: The first picture reminded me of the space unit we had last year. I remember pictures of the earth and moon taken from space like that picture.

    Mrs. Kinzinger: What area of the Brain Surfing sheet would that be?

    Tamika: It would be the science area.

    Mrs. Kinzinger: Let's write "space unit" in the science circle.

7. As you discuss students' connections with them, prompt them to think about areas of connections that they did not make. Provide them with your own connections if they are unable to make any. A sample discussion illustrating a prompt follows.

    Mrs. Kinzinger: No one made connections from *The Family of Earth* to music. Was anyone reminded of a song while they were reading?

    (No response.)

    Mrs. Kinzinger: Sometimes when I'm reading, music plays in my head. Often the music relates to the story, but sometimes it's a little different. When I was reading *The Family of Earth*, the song "We Are the World" came into my head. I've brought that song to play for you. [Play a recording of the song.] As you read, try to think of as many different kinds of connections as you can. If you "surf your brain," you'll be amazed at the different connections that you can make.

8. Encourage students to make connections on their own during and after reading. The Brain Surfing reproducible master can prompt students' attention to the various areas where they can connect their learning from the new book to their prior knowledge.

9. A sample Brain Surfing sheet for *The Family of Earth* and a reproducible master of the Brain Surfing graphic can be found on pages 14–16.

References

Lenski, S.D. (2001). Brain surfing: A strategy for making cross-curricular connections. *Reading Horizons, 42,* 21–37.

Schimmel, S. (2001). *The family of earth*. Minnetonka, MN: NorthWord Press.

Brain Surfing

The Family of Earth by S. Schimmel

Math
The earth is a sphere.
Weather unit

Science
Space unit
Animal habitats

Social Studies
Desert region
Rain forest

My life
Saw some of the animals at the zoo.
Saw a television special on Polar bears.

Language Arts
Wrote letters about rain forest.

Other books
Pole to Pole
Elephants
African Animals
Dolphins

Art
Photography

Music
"We Are the World"

Physical Education
Swimming in the ocean
Climbing mountains
Walking along the beach

Name _____ Date _____

📖 Brain Surfing

_____
Title and Author

Math

Science

Social Studies

My life

Language Arts

Other books

Art

Music

Physical Education

From Jerry L. Johns, Susan Davis Lenski, and Roberta L. Berglund, *Comprehension and Vocabulary Strategies for the Primary Grades*. Copyright © 2003 by Kendall/Hunt Publishing Company (1-800-247-3458, ext. 4 or 5). May be reproduced for noncommercial educational purposes within the guidelines noted on the copyright page.

Name _____ Date _____

Brain Surfing

Title and Author
_____

From Jerry L. Johns, Susan Davis Lenski, and Roberta L. Berglund, *Comprehension and Vocabulary Strategies for the Primary Grades*. Copyright © 2003 by Kendall/Hunt Publishing Company (1-800-247-3458, ext. 4 or 5). May be reproduced for noncommercial educational purposes within the guidelines noted on the copyright page.

CHARACTER FEELINGS

FOCUS		TEXT		WHEN			WHY									HOW			
Comprehension	Vocabulary	Narrative	Informational	Before Reading	During Reading	After Reading	Predicting	Connecting	Questioning	Using Text Structure	Visualizing	Inferring	Summarizing	Synthesizing	Determining Importance	Individual	Partner	Small Group	Whole Group
●		●				●					●	●		●		●		●	●

Description

Character Feelings, based on Johns and Berglund (2002) and Johns and Lenski (2001), can be used with fictional characters, real people, or biographical sketches. Students' identification of the feelings should be based on an analysis of the printed material. Students should also provide evidence for their decisions.

Procedure

1. Identify a particular short, narrative reading selection that can be read with or to students. When doing this activity for the first time, you may want to choose a selection that has only one main character. Kindergarten and first-grade teachers may want to have a Big Book to read to the students. Second- and third-grade teachers may want to provide either a personal copy of the selection for students or use a large copy with the entire class.

2. Draw or show a picture of a smiley face. Ask students what a smiley face represents. They may say happiness or joy. Accept any reasonable answer and write the word on the board or an overhead transparency.

3. Ask the students to think of any faces they can make that would show how a person might feel. Call on a student to show his or her face to the class without saying anything. Have the other students "guess" what face is being presented, draw that face, and write an appropriate feeling word on the board. You may want to draw the faces with other emotions and write the feeling word next to it. Continue with this activity until students have made all the faces they can think of at that time. Some possibilities are listed in the sidebar to the right.

4. Have students read the selection or read the selection to them. After reading the selection, have students draw (or circle) the face(s) they think represents the feelings of the character. This can be done on the reproducible master or on the board. Older students can write a short reminder of clues in the story. A face could be drawn in the margin next to the text that supports the feeling.

5. If your reading selection has several characters, you might also have students discuss the feelings of those characters.

References

Johns, J.L., & Berglund, R.L. (2002). *Strategies for content area learning.* Dubuque, IA: Kendall/Hunt.

Johns, J.L., & Lenski, S.D. (2001). *Improving reading: Strategies and resources* (3rd ed.). Dubuque, IA: Kendall/Hunt.

📖 Character Feelings

DIRECTIONS Choose a character in the story. Circle the word that tells how the character in the story felt and draw the face to show that feeling.

Character's Name _____

Happy	Sad	Mad
Scared		Very Sad

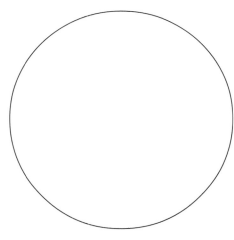

Happy	Sad	Mad
Scared		Very Sad

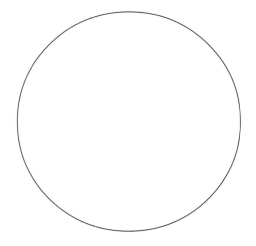

Happy	Sad	Mad
Scared		Very Sad

CHARACTER FOUR SQUARE

FOCUS		TEXT		WHEN			WHY									HOW			
Comprehension	Vocabulary	Narrative	Informational	Before Reading	During Reading	After Reading	Predicting	Connecting	Questioning	Using Text Structure	Visualizing	Inferring	Summarizing	Synthesizing	Determining Importance	Individual	Partner	Small Group	Whole Group
●	●	●				●		●			●					●	●	●	●

Description

Character Four Square is a strategy to help teach or review characterization in a story. Students may make inferences to come up with some of the information requested. The information is then placed in four squares.

Procedure

1. Choose a book or story with a character (person or animal) that will be relatively easy for students to describe. Initially, use a short text with one main character to read to the entire class.

2. Make an overhead transparency of the reproducible master on page 23 or draw a square with four quadrants on the board. Label them as shown in the example below. For younger students, you may wish to use the reproducible master on page 24.

Name	Physical Description
Feelings	**Character Traits**

3. Before reading the story, it may be helpful to relate aspects of Character Four Square to yourself. You may want to invite students to share their ideas, so you can help them distinguish between feelings and traits.

4. Explain the procedure and the words in each quadrant. You might say the following.

> Look at the words in each of these squares. Let's talk about what these words mean. Stories have characters. They can be people or animals. After I read *The Bird, the Frog, and the Light* (Avi, 1994), we will write the name of a character here. [Point to the appropriate square in each case.] In the next square, we will list words that tell what the character looks like—what I would see if I looked with my eyes. As I read, think of some feelings the character may have. We'll want to list those here. Then talk about the traits characters can have, such as honesty.

5. After reading the story, invite students to decide which character to write in the top left quadrant. Then add any physical description students can remember from the story. You may want to read certain parts of the story again to help students recall descriptions, feelings, and traits. Systematically complete the Character Four Square, offering clarification as needed. Below is a completed example for *The Bird, the Frog, and the Light*.

Name	Physical Description
Frog	yellow toes big green bulging wore a crown
Feelings important sad	**Character Traits** bossy proud mean impatient

6. Be sure to help students understand that most feelings and traits must be inferred from what the characters say and do. Below is an example.

> Mr. Lane: You did a great job describing how Frog looked by using the pictures and what the author actually said. But when we list feelings and traits, the author may not actually say the words. We have to infer or guess what the author might have in mind from the story. Who has an idea for a word that describes Frog's character? Be sure and tell why you think so. What is your evidence?

Cherrith: I think Frog was bossy. He ordered Bird around.

Corey: Frog was also proud. The story said he puffed himself up. The picture also showed him puffed up.

Max: I think being puffed up was Frog's way to feel important. You can tell that Frog wanted to feel important from the way he acted.

Josh: Frog was also mean. I didn't like the way he talked to Bird. He ordered Bird around, and Mr. Lane sounded mean when he read that part of the story.

Mr. Lane: You have shared some appropriate traits and feelings for Frog. I especially liked how you used your ideas along with the story to come up with words.

7. If the story or selection has other characters, they may be discussed using another Character Four Square. For example, Character Four Square can be completed for Bird and Light in *The Bird, the Frog, and the Light*.

8. When students understand the strategy, have them work in small groups, with partners, or individually. Young students may draw pictures for the character and some of the feelings and descriptions. Reproducible masters can be found on pages 23 and 24.

Reference

Avi. (1994). *The Bird, the Frog, and the Light*. New York: Overland Books.

Name _____ Date _____

 # Character Four Square

Name	Physical Description

Feelings	Character Traits

From Jerry L. Johns, Susan Davis Lenski, and Roberta L. Berglund, *Comprehension and Vocabulary Strategies for the Primary Grades*. Copyright © 2003 by Kendall/Hunt Publishing Company (1-800-247-3458, ext. 4 or 5). May be reproduced for noncommercial educational purposes within the guidelines noted on the copyright page.

Character Four Square

My character's name	Words that tell how my character looks
Feelings my character shows or has	**A drawing of my character showing traits**

From Jerry L. Johns, Susan Davis Lenski, and Roberta L. Berglund, *Comprehension and Vocabulary Strategies for the Primary Grades*. Copyright © 2003 by Kendall/Hunt Publishing Company (1-800-247-3458, ext. 4 or 5). May be reproduced for noncommercial educational purposes within the guidelines noted on the copyright page.

CONCEPT CIRCLES

FOCUS		TEXT		WHEN			WHY									HOW			
Comprehension	Vocabulary	Narrative	Informational	Before Reading	During Reading	After Reading	Predicting	Connecting	Questioning	Using Text Structure	Visualizing	Inferring	Summarizing	Synthesizing	Determining Importance	Individual	Partner	Small Group	Whole Group
	●		●			●						●		●	●	●	●		

Description

Concept Circles (Vacca & Vacca, 2003) provide opportunities for students to think about how words and their related concepts are connected. Concept Circles are intriguing to students because they have an opportunity to classify words in a visual way. This strategy is often viewed by students as "fun," while providing an opportunity for them to extend their understanding of words and terms they are learning.

There are three ways to work with Concept Circles. The first asks students to view a completed circle containing two to four words or phrases and then identify the concept represented by the words or phrases in the circle. In a second pattern, one or two of the segments of the circle are left empty, and students are invited to add words and/or pictures that fit the concept. Students may also be asked to name the concept. The third way of using Concept Circles is to ask students to identify a word or phrase in the circle that does not belong. Students can also be asked to replace the word or phrase that doesn't belong with one that fits the overall concept. All of the ways of working with Concept Circles involve students in thinking about how words relate to each other and how they relate to a superordinate concept. Concept Circles can serve as a quick and meaningful review of ideas and also as a way to help students begin to think about how words and concepts are alike or different.

Procedure

1. Select the type of Concept Circle you wish to introduce to your students. Make a transparency of the appropriate reproducible master (see pages 27–28) and display it on an overhead projector. Tell students that this type of graphic can help them think about the meanings of some of the words they are learning and how the words may be connected.

2. Model the use of Concept Circles by choosing well-understood concepts and inviting the class to participate in completing the circles with you. For example, the words in the circle might be *Brown Bear, Charlotte's Web,* and *Clifford, The Big Red Dog.* Ask students, "What is the big idea that includes all of these words?"

Students should offer ideas such as "books" or "names of books in our classroom library." Write the category they select on the line above the circle and help students understand that the category includes all the words in the circle.

3. After students have become familiar with the first way of using Concept Circles, choose to model a circle where the words included might be *flag* and *chalkboard* and one segment is left blank. Ask, "How are these words connected?" Students might say, "They are things in our classroom." Write the response on the line at the top of the transparency. Ask, "What word could you add to our circle that fits our title?" Students might suggest, *clock, book shelves, desks,* or *tables.* Choose one and write it in the blank section of the circle.

4. After students have become familiar with the first two uses of Concept Circles, show students a completed circle in which one of the words included in the circle does not fit the concept. Have students read the words in this circle. Then say, "One of the words doesn't belong. Can you tell me which one doesn't belong and why you think so?"

   An example might be *banana, apple, candy bar.* After students identify *candy bar* as the word that doesn't fit, cross out the word or shade in that section of the circle on the transparency with an overhead marking pen. Then ask students to identify the concept *fruit* and ask them to suggest a replacement for *candy bar* that does fit the concept. Students might suggest *orange* or *pear.* Write the new word in the circle.

5. After modeling the strategy, give students an opportunity to complete Concept Circles independently. You may want to invite students to work individually or in pairs to complete Concept Circle activities. Have them use circles you have developed or give students blank copies of the appropriate reproducible master on pages 29–31. Ask them to create circles using words from a lesson or unit of study that is ongoing in your classroom.

6. When the circles are completed, have students share some of their ideas or transfer them to a transparency and present them to the rest of the class. Their peers will enjoy matching wits with the circles' creators by guessing the categories, suggesting other words that might relate to the category, or reviewing the words that don't "fit" those in the circle.

Reference

Vacca, R.T., & Vacca, J.L. (2003). *Content area reading: Literacy and learning across the curriculum* (7th ed.). Boston: Allyn and Bacon.

Concept Circles

DIRECTIONS
1. Read the words in each circle.
2. Think of a word or phrase that tells how they are all alike.
3. Write that word or phrase on the line above the circle.

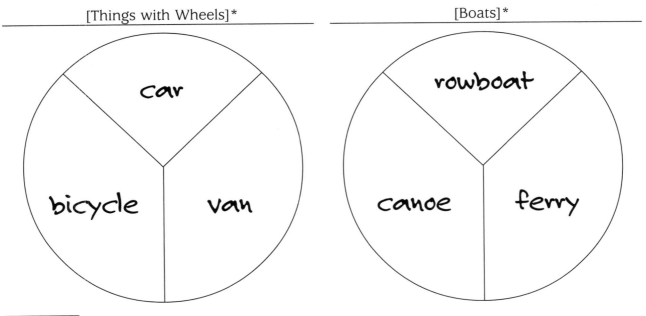

_____ [Things with Wheels]* _____

car

bicycle   van

_____ [Boats]* _____

rowboat

canoe   ferry

DIRECTIONS
1. Read the words in each circle.
2. Think of a word or phrase that tells how they are all alike.
3. Write that word or phrase on the line above the circle.
4. Now add a word or phrase to the circle that fits with the others.

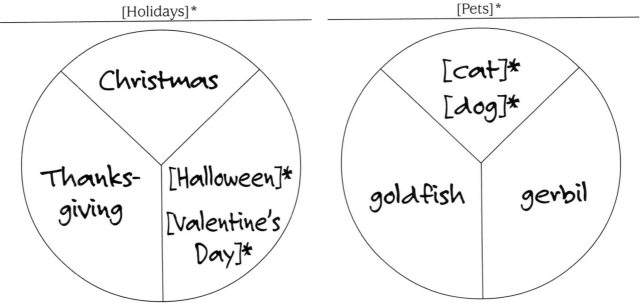

_____ [Holidays]* _____

Christmas

Thanks-giving   [Halloween]* [Valentine's Day]*

_____ [Pets]* _____

[cat]* [dog]*

goldfish   gerbil

*Brackets [ ] indicate possible student responses.

From Jerry L. Johns, Susan Davis Lenski, and Roberta L. Berglund, _Comprehension and Vocabulary Strategies for the Primary Grades_. Copyright © 2003 by Kendall/Hunt Publishing Company (1-800-247-3458, ext. 4 or 5). May be reproduced for noncommercial educational purposes within the guidelines noted on the copyright page.

Concept Circles

DIRECTIONS
1. Read the words in each circle. One of them doesn't belong. Draw a line through it.
2. Think of a word or phrase that tells how the other words are alike. Write that word or phrase on the line above the circle.
3. Replace the word you have crossed out with a word or phrase that *does* belong with the others in the circle. Write it in the circle.

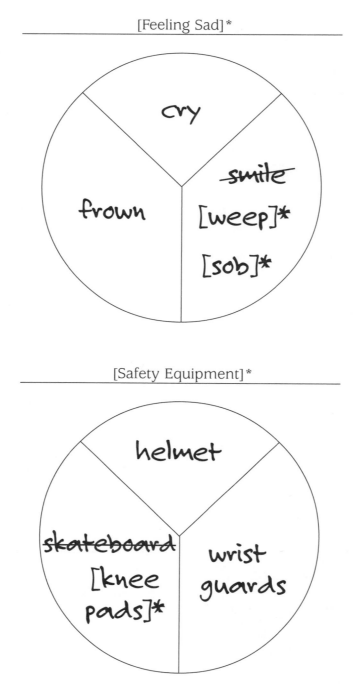

[Feeling Sad]*

cry

~~smile~~
[weep]*
[sob]*

frown

[Safety Equipment]*

helmet

~~skateboard~~
[knee pads]*

wrist guards

*Brackets [   ] indicate possible student responses.

From Jerry L. Johns, Susan Davis Lenski, and Roberta L. Berglund, *Comprehension and Vocabulary Strategies for the Primary Grades*. Copyright © 2003 by Kendall/Hunt Publishing Company (1-800-247-3458, ext. 4 or 5). May be reproduced for noncommercial educational purposes within the guidelines noted on the copyright page.

 # Concept Circles

_____
(topic)

DIRECTIONS
1. Read the words in each circle.
2. Think of a word or phrase that tells how they are all alike.
3. Write that word or phrase on the line above the circle.

_____

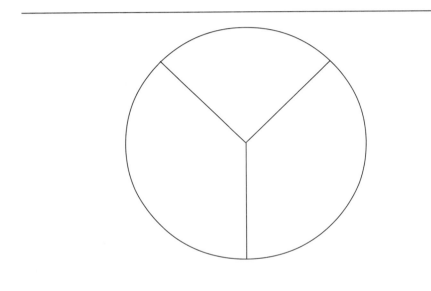

_____

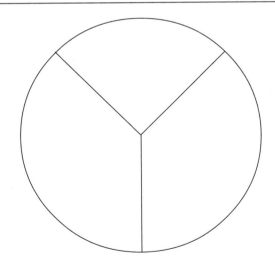

Based on Vacca, R.T., & Vacca, J.L. (2003). *Content area reading: Literacy and learning across the curriculum* (7th ed.). Boston: Allyn and Bacon.

From Jerry L. Johns, Susan Davis Lenski, and Roberta L. Berglund, *Comprehension and Vocabulary Strategies for the Primary Grades*. Copyright © 2003 by Kendall/Hunt Publishing Company (1-800-247-3458, ext. 4 or 5). May be reproduced for noncommercial educational purposes within the guidelines noted on the copyright page.

Name _____ Date _____

 # Concept Circles

_____
(topic)

DIRECTIONS
1. Read the words in each circle.
2. Think of a word or phrase that tells how they are all alike.
3. Write that word or phrase on the line above the circle.
4. Think of a word or phrase that fits with the others in the circle.
5. Write your word or phrase in the circle.

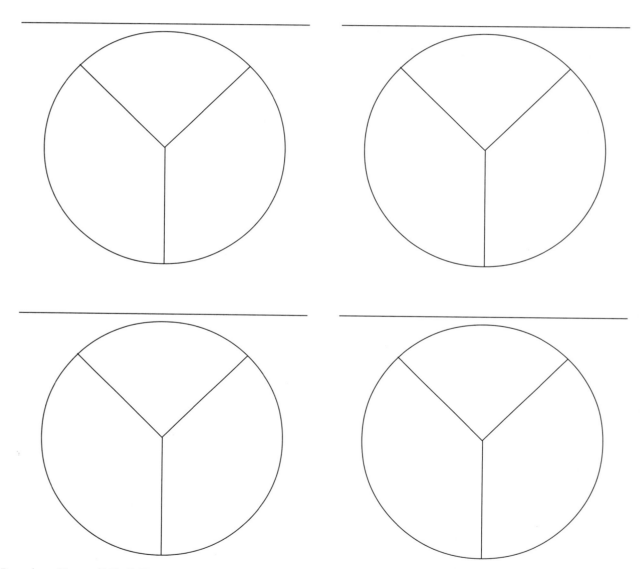

Based on Vacca, R.T., & Vacca, J.L. (2003). *Content area reading: Literacy and learning across the curriculum* (7th ed.). Boston: Allyn and Bacon.

From Jerry L. Johns, Susan Davis Lenski, and Roberta L. Berglund, *Comprehension and Vocabulary Strategies for the Primary Grades*. Copyright © 2003 by Kendall/Hunt Publishing Company (1-800-247-3458, ext. 4 or 5). May be reproduced for noncommercial educational purposes within the guidelines noted on the copyright page.

Name _____ Date _____

 # Concept Circles

_____
(topic)

DIRECTIONS
1. Read the words in each circle. One of them doesn't belong. Draw a line through it.
2. Think of a word or phrase that tells how the words are alike. Write that word or phrase on the line above the circle.
3. Replace the word you have crossed out with a word or phrase that *does* belong with the others in the circle. Write it in the circle.

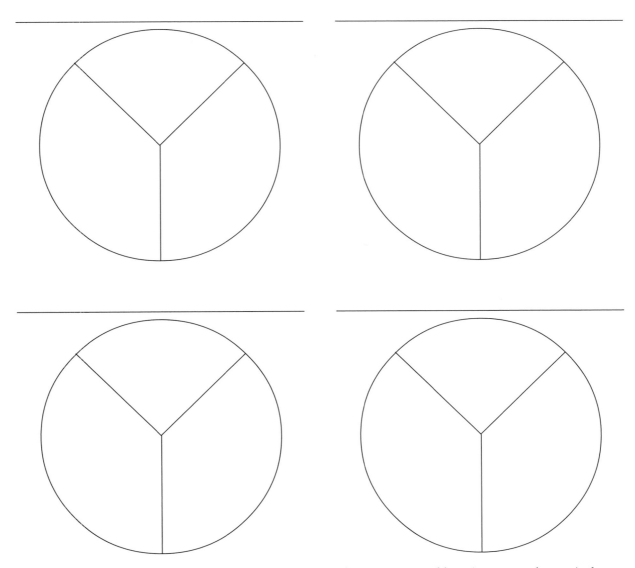

Based on Vacca, R.T., & Vacca, J.L. (2003). *Content area reading: Literacy and learning across the curriculum* (7th ed.). Boston: Allyn and Bacon.

From Jerry L. Johns, Susan Davis Lenski, and Roberta L. Berglund, *Comprehension and Vocabulary Strategies for the Primary Grades*. Copyright © 2003 by Kendall/Hunt Publishing Company (1-800-247-3458, ext. 4 or 5). May be reproduced for noncommercial educational purposes within the guidelines noted on the copyright page.

CUBING

FOCUS		TEXT		WHEN			WHY									HOW			
Comprehension	Vocabulary	Narrative	Informational	Before Reading	During Reading	After Reading	Predicting	Connecting	Questioning	Using Text Structure	Visualizing	Inferring	Summarizing	Synthesizing	Determining Importance	Individual	Partner	Small Group	Whole Group
●	●	●	●			●		●	●	●	●	●		●	●		●	●	

Description

Cubing is a comprehension strategy that will help young students recall the main parts of a story. It provides a structure to help students acquire knowledge of the major parts of a story to be discussed. More advanced uses of Cubing can encourage critical thinking and analysis (Cowen & Cowen, 1980). There are several variations of cubing, and reproducible masters are provided for each of them.

Procedure

1. Choose a short piece of literature that will lend itself to easily discussing the different parts of a story. These would include the following: title, characters, setting, problem, key events, and solution.

2. Read the story in a large group, small groups, pairs, or alone. Have a large cube already assembled or use a box. As you discuss each part, write the descriptive word and the example from the story. After reading *Come On, Rain!* (Hesse, 1999) you might say the following.

    > Look at this box I am holding. It has six sides with a word or phrase on each side. The box has the major parts that make up the story we just read. [Show the part of the cube with *title* and have a student share the title. Do the same with the other parts of the cube elaborating and explaining as necessary.]

3. After modeling the cube with the entire class, have students make a cube from the reproducible master on page 34. For younger students, you may need to have the cubes already made. You may also find that small blocks of wood can serve as durable and easy-to-make cubes.

4. Once the cubes are prepared, you might say the following.

> A box with six sides is called a cube. Your cube has the major parts that make up stories. After we read a story, we may sometimes review it by using our cubes. If you remember the parts of the cube, they can help you recall the important parts of many stories. Let's try the cube with this story. [Identify the story.]

5. Have students read the new story in small groups or with partners. After reading, students can roll the cube and take turns responding. Cubing can also serve as an assessment of students' understanding of the main parts of a story, as well as a review technique.

6. An alternative would be to adapt the cube for biographical information about people studied in your curriculum. The sides of the cube could contain the following information.

   - name, birthplace
   - a struggle the person experienced
   - a fact about the person
   - why this person is remembered
   - something you admire about the person
   - a special accomplishment

You might use student autobiographies to help get students familiar with this cube before using the basic framework for biographies. An added benefit of using the "autobiographical" cube with students is that they can get to know each other better.

7. Older students can be introduced to a problem/issue cube that encourages them to examine a topic or area from various sides or viewpoints. The sides of the cube would contain the following elements.

   - describe it (process, events, features, traits)
   - compare it (similarities/differences)
   - associate it (connections, analogies)
   - apply it (link to other situations, experiences, events)
   - analyze it (composition, procedures, steps)
   - argue for or against it (take a position)

Students could be invited to share their ideas orally or with brief notes. If ideas are written, there should be time for discussion. It is often helpful to limit the time spent on each element of the cube.

References

Hesse, K. (1999). *Come on, rain!* New York: Scholastic.

Cowen, G., & Cowen, E. (1980). *Writing.* New York: Wiley.

Story Cube

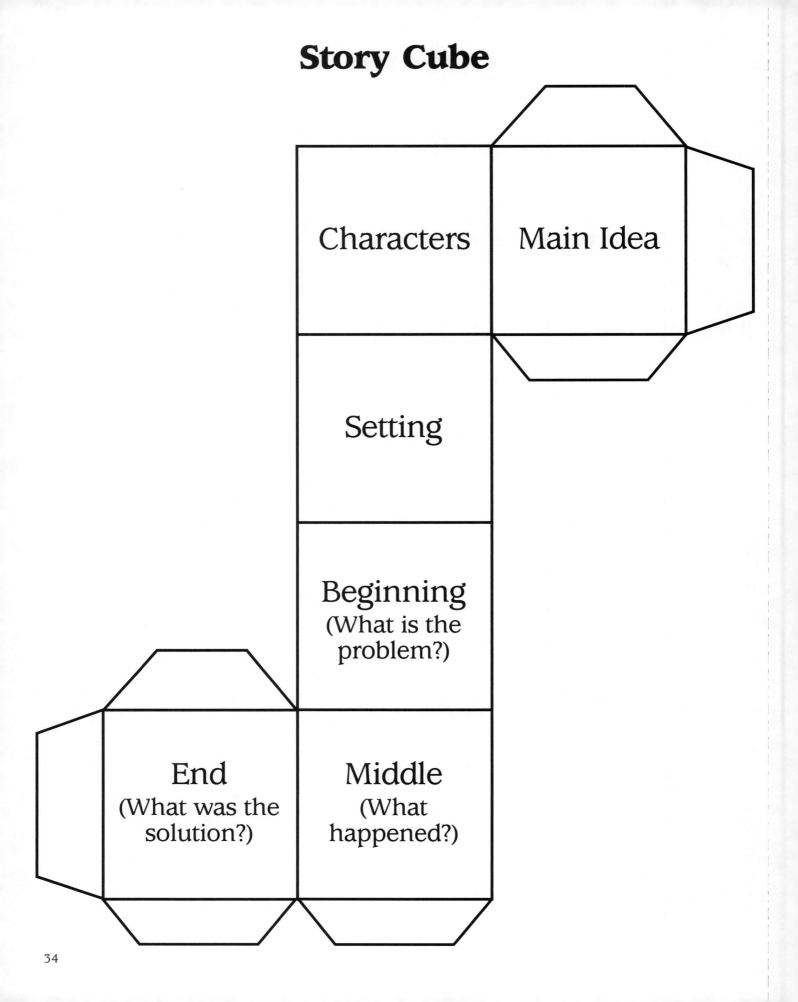

Characters

Main Idea

Setting

Beginning
(What is the
problem?)

End
(What was the
solution?)

Middle
(What
happened?)

Story Cube

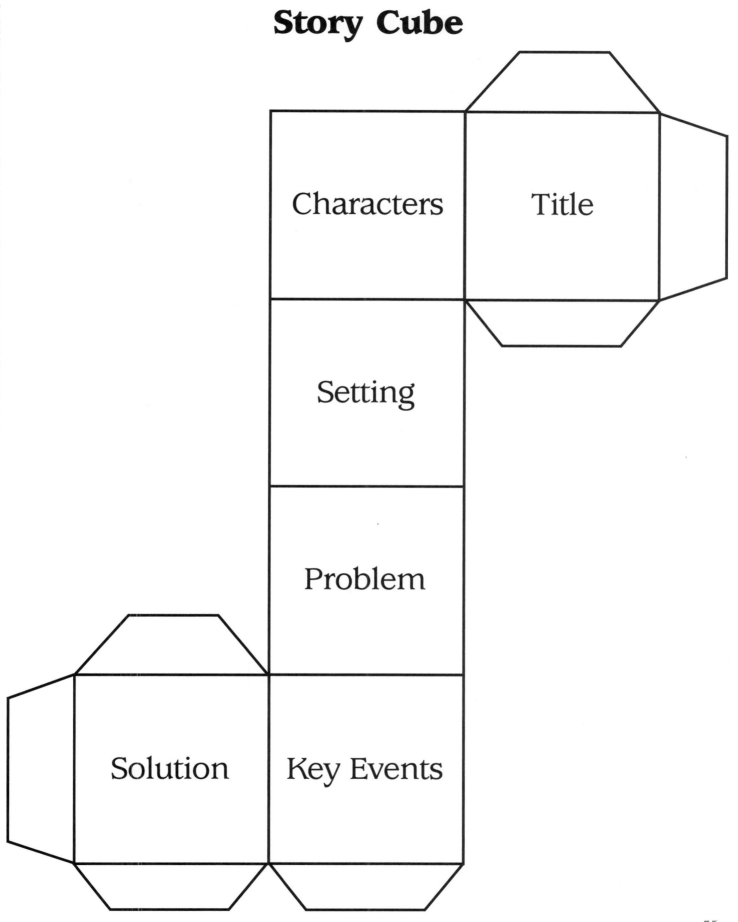

Biography Cube

A struggle the person had

Name and birthplace

A fact about the person

Why this person is remembered

A special accomplish-ment

Something you admire about the person

Problem/Issue Cube

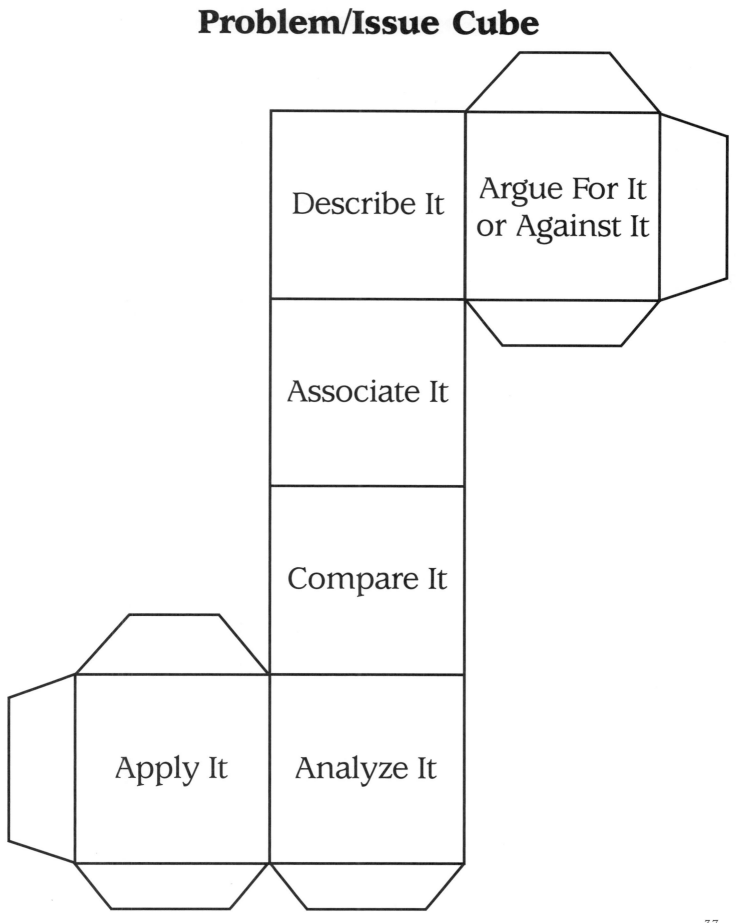

Autobiography Cube

Month born | Birthplace

A favorite food

A memory

A special accomplish-ment | A favorite person

DIRECTED READING-THINKING ACTIVITY (DR-TA) DIRECTED LISTENING-THINKING ACTIVITY (DL-TA)

FOCUS		TEXT		WHEN			WHY									HOW			
Comprehension	Vocabulary	Narrative	Informational	Before Reading	During Reading	After Reading	Predicting	Connecting	Questioning	Using Text Structure	Visualizing	Inferring	Summarizing	Synthesizing	Determining Importance	Individual	Partner	Small Group	Whole Group
●		●		●	●	●	●	●	●			●						●	

Description

The Directed Reading-Thinking Activity (DR-TA) (Stauffer, 1975) and its companion strategy, the Directed Listening-Thinking Activity (DL-TA) (Richek, 1987), help students become critical readers or listeners as they make and check predictions about the content of a text. While the DR-TA and DL-TA can be used with informational text, they are most often introduced and used with narrative text. The DR-TA and DL-TA help students set purposes for reading or listening, understand information, actively read or listen to a text, and check the accuracy of predictions made about its content.

Procedure

1. Select a book or story that can elicit rich predictions. A selection with a well-defined plot and events, as well as a surprise ending, are often useful in introducing this strategy.

2. Prior to introducing the book or story to students, choose a small number of stopping points in the text. These points could be related to major events in the story or those that will encourage reflection and conjecture about the meaning of the text.

3. Invite students to look at the title or cover of the reading material and answer the following question.

    What do you think this book (or story) is going to be about?

    Provide opportunities for several students to respond. You may want to record their predictions on the board or on chart paper. As students offer predictions, follow each by asking, "Why?" or "What makes you think so?" Allow several students to make predictions and explain their thinking.

4. In order to involve all students in making predictions and setting purposes for reading or listening, ask those students who have not actively made predictions to raise their hands indicating which prediction they agree with. You might say the following.

   Jenny, we have three predictions written on the board. Which one do you think is the best prediction for what our story is going to be about?

5. In some situations you might use the following options. Read each prediction aloud and have students raise their hands to indicate their choice. For younger students, after three or four predictions are given, have the children who contributed the predictions move to different corners of the room. Have the remaining students go and stand with the person whose prediction they agree with. Repeat this process after each stopping point in the selection.

6. When several predictions have been made, ask students to read or listen until a predetermined stopping point in the text has been reached. Then ask students to reconsider their predictions.

   Were your predictions correct? Why or why not? [Invite several students to explain their thinking.]

7. When several of the predictions have been discussed, ask students if they wish to change their predictions and/or make new ones. Again, ask them to explain their reasoning.

8. Continue with the prediction, read (or listen), and prove cycle until enough information has been presented for the ideas to begin to converge. At this point, finish the story.

9. At the completion of the story, follow-up with reading (or listening) response activities, word study, meaningful rereading, or concept development. Reproducible masters on pages 41 and 42 are for use in a reading or listening center in the classroom.

References

Richek, M.A. (1987). DR-TA: 5 variations that facilitate independence in reading narratives. *Journal of Reading, 30,* 632–636.

Stauffer, R.E. (1975). *Directing the reading-thinking process.* New York: Harper & Row.

 # Thinking about My Reading or Listening

Before you read or listen, draw a picture showing what you think the story will be about.

Were you right? Why or why not? Change your picture or draw a new one showing your ideas about the story now.

From Jerry L. Johns, Susan Davis Lenski, and Roberta L. Berglund, *Comprehension and Vocabulary Strategies for the Primary Grades*. Copyright © 2003 by Kendall/Hunt Publishing Company (1-800-247-3458, ext. 4 or 5). May be reproduced for noncommercial educational purposes within the guidelines noted on the copyright page.

It is important to keep thinking as you read or listen. Remember to ask yourself these questions.

What is this going to be about?

What makes me think so?

Was I right? Why or why not?

How could I change my ideas to match what I know so far?

What will happen next?

What makes me think so?

From Jerry L. Johns, Susan Davis Lenski, and Roberta L. Berglund, *Comprehension and Vocabulary Strategies for the Primary Grades*. Copyright © 2003 by Kendall/Hunt Publishing Company (1-800-247-3458, ext. 4 or 5). May be reproduced for noncommercial educational purposes within the guidelines noted on the copyright page.

FINDING MY OWN WORDS

FOCUS		TEXT		WHEN			WHY									HOW			
Comprehension	Vocabulary	Narrative	Informational	Before Reading	During Reading	After Reading	Predicting	Connecting	Questioning	Using Text Structure	Visualizing	Inferring	Summarizing	Synthesizing	Determining Importance	Individual	Partner	Small Group	Whole Group
	●	●	●			●		●							●	●	●	●	●

Description

Students will learn new vocabulary terms through instruction, but they should also be encouraged to discover new words while they are reading independently. One strategy that helps students become aware of new words while reading is Finding My Own Words, an adaptation of the Vocabulary Self-Collection Strategy (VSS) (Haggard, 1986). Finding My Own Words heightens students' awareness of unfamiliar words and provides them with practice in learning new words in their natural contexts.

Procedure

1. Tell students that they learn new words in many ways and that independent reading is one of the ways students can learn new words. Emphasize that knowing the meanings of many words will help students become better readers. Also explain that becoming aware of new words can enrich students' vocabularies.

2. Explain to students that there is a strategy that can help them become aware of words as they read: Finding My Own Words. Write the name of the strategy on the board.

3. To begin this strategy, demonstrate how to independently look for new words in reading. An example that you could use follows.

    > I was reading the book *Emily* (Bedard, 1992) last night because I wanted to read it to our class. It's a children's book about the poet Emily Dickinson. As I read the book, I came to a word that I didn't know: *parlor*. I had heard the word many times, but I wasn't exactly sure what it meant. I decided that the word *parlor* was a word that I wanted to learn. I also thought it would be a good one for our entire class to learn.

4. After you have modeled finding a new word, provide students with a story to read that has some unfamiliar words. Have students read the book and write down words that intrigued them. For example, if students read the story *Emily*, they might choose the following words: *plucked*, *wilted*, *hedge*, *bulged*, and *rascal*.

5. Divide the class into groups of three or four students. Have students share their lists of individually selected words with their group and instruct the group to choose one word to present to the rest of the class.

6. Have each group share the word that they selected. Write the words on the board or on an overhead transparency. Conduct a vote for one word from the list for the class to learn.

7. Duplicate and distribute the Finding My Own Words reproducible master on page 45. After students have selected a word from the class list, have them find the word in its context in the story and write it on the sheet. Then have students predict a definition from the context in which the word occurs. Finally, have them check on the accuracy of their definition with a dictionary or glossary. An example follows.

Word	Sentence Where I Found the Word
Parlor	"Glasses chimed through the open parlor door below."
Predicted Definition	**Definition**
A living room	A room used for visitors.

8. Encourage students to use a Finding My Own Words sheet while reading to record new vocabulary words using the reproducible master on page 45.

References

Bedard, M. (1992). *Emily*. New York: Scholastic.

Haggard, M.R. (1986). The vocabulary self-collection strategy: Using student interest and word knowledge to enhance vocabulary growth. *Journal of Reading, 29*, 634–642.

Finding My Own Words

Name _____

Date _____

Word _____

Predicted Definition _____

Sentence Where I Found the Word _____

Definition _____

Word _____

Predicted Definition _____

Sentence Where I Found the Word _____

Definition _____

Word _____

Predicted Definition _____

Sentence Where I Found the Word _____

Definition _____

Based on Haggard, M.R. (1986). The vocabulary self-collection strategy: Using student interest and word knowledge to enhance vocabulary growth. *Journal of Reading, 29,* 634–642.

From Jerry L. Johns, Susan Davis Lenski, and Roberta L. Berglund, *Comprehension and Vocabulary Strategies for the Primary Grades.* Copyright © 2003 by Kendall/Hunt Publishing Company (1-800-247-3458, ext. 4 or 5). May be reproduced for noncommercial educational purposes within the guidelines noted on the copyright page.

FOUR SQUARE

FOCUS		TEXT		WHEN			WHY									HOW			
Comprehension	Vocabulary	Narrative	Informational	Before Reading	During Reading	After Reading	Predicting	Connecting	Questioning	Using Text Structure	Visualizing	Inferring	Summarizing	Synthesizing	Determining Importance	Individual	Partner	Small Group	Whole Group
	●	●	●			●		●		●						●	●	●	●

Description

Four Square, as described in Johns and Berglund (2002) and Lenski, Wham, and Johns (2003), is a vocabulary strategy to help students learn meanings for words. One key element of the strategy is having students make a personal association or connection with the word. Such a connection may enhance vocabulary acquisition and aid in the retrieval of the word's meaning when it is encountered in print.

Procedure

1. Draw a square with four quadrants on the board or chart paper. Label each of the quadrants as shown in the example below. For older students, you can make an overhead transparency of the appropriate Four Square reproducible master.

Word	My Connection
What It Means	**Picture or How It Looks**

2. Model the strategy using a vocabulary word selected from a text students will read or use the example from *Weather Tools* (Lowell, 2003) below. You might model the strategy by saying the following.

> Today we will be reading a book about things that can help us learn about the weather. I've selected a word from the book. [Print *thermometer* in the upper-left quadrant and invite a student to pronounce the word.] Notice that there are three other squares on the chart. [Point out the squares.] When we complete the four squares, you will know more about the word.

3. Then have students share their ideas about the word's meanings. Following the reading of the book, write a brief definition of *thermometer* in the lower-left quadrant of the Four Square and read the definition to the group.

4. Have a student read the phrase in the lower-right quadrant. Then have students share descriptions of *thermometer* that could be used to draw a picture or an illustration. When the sharing is completed, make a sketch of a *thermometer* in the lower-right quadrant. A student could also be asked to draw the illustration.

5. For the upper-right quadrant, tell students something like the following.

> To help you remember *thermometer,* make a personal connection or clue to help you remember the word. Each of you may have a different connection. My connection is that we have an indoor/outdoor thermometer in our home. What personal connection can you make with *thermometer* or what helps you think of *thermometer*? [Have students share their connections in small groups or with a partner. Then ask for volunteers to share with the class. Stress that connections, by their very nature, can be unique and personal.]

Word	My Connection
thermometer	We have an indoor/outdoor thermometer at home.
What It Means	**Picture or How It Looks**
It tells how hot or cold it is.	

6. Use Four Square several more times with the whole class to help students gain a working knowledge of the strategy. When students gain confidence with the strategy, share copies of the reproducible master on page 49 with students and guide them in completing the sheet individually or in small groups. Words chosen should be important in understanding the lesson you are teaching. The terms *rain gauge* and *wind sock*, for example, might be possible words for a unit on weather tools.

7. One variation of Four Square is to substitute *Opposite* for *Picture or How It Looks* in the bottom-right quadrant. The reproducible master on page 50 contains this option, so you can choose the reproducible master that is most appropriate for your use.

References

Johns, J.L., & Berglund, R.L. (2002). *Strategies for content area learning.* Dubuque, IA: Kendall/Hunt.

Lenski, S.D., Wham, M.A., & Johns, J.L. (2003). *Reading & learning strategies: Middle grades through high school* (2nd ed.). Dubuque, IA: Kendall/Hunt.

Lowell, M. (2003). *Weather tools.* New York: Sadlier-Oxford.

Name _____ Date _____

 **Four Square**

Word	My Connection

What It Means	Picture or How It Looks

From Jerry L. Johns, Susan Davis Lenski, and Roberta L. Berglund, *Comprehension and Vocabulary Strategies for the Primary Grades*. Copyright © 2003 by Kendall/Hunt Publishing Company (1-800-247-3458, ext. 4 or 5). May be reproduced for noncommercial educational purposes within the guidelines noted on the copyright page.

 **Four Square**

Word	Personal Clue or Connection
Definition	Opposite

From Jerry L. Johns, Susan Davis Lenski, and Roberta L. Berglund, *Comprehension and Vocabulary Strategies for the Primary Grades*. Copyright © 2003 by Kendall/Hunt Publishing Company (1-800-247-3458, ext. 4 or 5). May be reproduced for noncommercial educational purposes within the guidelines noted on the copyright page.

GETTING THE RIGHT ORDER

FOCUS		TEXT		WHEN			WHY									HOW			
Comprehension	Vocabulary	Narrative	Informational	Before Reading	During Reading	After Reading	Predicting	Connecting	Questioning	Using Text Structure	Visualizing	Inferring	Summarizing	Synthesizing	Determining Importance	Individual	Partner	Small Group	Whole Group
●		●	●			●				●					●	●	●	●	●

Description

Informational texts are organized around recognizable text structures in the same way narrative texts are. Narrative texts have a story grammar; they all have the elements: setting, characters, plot, and theme. The structure of informational texts is different. Informational texts are usually organized by sequence, main idea/details, comparison/contrast, problem/solution, or cause/effect. Similar to narrative texts, when students understand how an informational text is organized, their comprehension improves. A strategy that helps students understand how sequential texts are organized is Getting the Right Order based on the Sequence Idea Map (Armbruster, 1986). Getting the Right Order is a graphic organizer that helps students identify events in a sequence in both narrative and informational text.

Procedure

1. Tell students that some books are written with events that take place in a sequence or order. Write the word *sequence* on the board and have students say the word aloud with you. Explain that the word *sequence* means that events take place in a specific order.

2. Illustrate the meaning of the word *sequence* by telling a story similar to the following.

   > I'm going to describe what I mean by the word *sequence* by telling you about the day I gave my dog, Zeke, a bath. Here are the steps I took, in the order that they happened. First, I ran warm water in the washtub. Then I tried to find my dog. Zeke hid under the couch, but I caught him. After that, I carried him to the washtub. I turned on the water and soaped him up real good. I rinsed him off and toweled him dry. Then he shook himself and got me all wet!

3. Explain to students that the story had events that happened in a specific order. Ask students to remember the events in order and write them on chart paper or the board similar to the following.

   1. I ran warm water in the washtub.
   2. I tried to find my dog, Zeke.

3. Zeke hid under the couch.
4. I caught him.
5. I carried him to the washtub.
6. I turned on the water.
7. I soaped him up.
8. I rinsed him.
9. I toweled him dry.
10. Zeke shook himself and got me wet.

4. Tell students that when they find a sequence of events in reading, they should pay attention to the order of the events. Explain to students that identifying the sequence of events will help them better understand and remember the story.

5. Duplicate and distribute the sample idea maps that follow on pages 53–54, or provide students with your own examples of idea maps using both narrative and informational texts.

6. Read one of the texts to students and show them in the story or passage where each different event occurred. As you show students the events in the text, draw their attention to the statement listed on the sequence idea map. Explain that as they read an event in their text they should write it in one of the idea map boxes.

7. After students have practiced locating a sequence of events by the sample idea maps, duplicate and distribute the reproducible master of Getting the Right Order on page 55.

8. Remind students that good readers try to find the organizational pattern of the book they are reading. Then have students work in small groups or individually to find the sequence of events in their reading.

References

Armbruster, B.B. (1986, December). *Using frames to organize expository text*. Paper presented at the annual meeting of the National Reading Conference, Austin, TX.

Feiffer, J. (2001). *I'm not Bobby!* Manhasset, NY: Hyperion.

Riley, K. (1988). *Dreamers and their dreams*. New York: Scholastic.

Now let's look at another word from our reading. This one is *tundra*. Let's see, I know I have seen and heard it before. So I think I will put my "x" under *Think I Know It*. I think I know what this word means, but I'll need to read and find out if I am right.

5. Display the next word and invite a student to come to the board or overhead projector and show where he or she would put an "x" indicating his or her familiarity with the word. Invite the student to explain why he or she marked the word in a particular column.

6. When students appear to be comfortable with the How Well Do I Know These Words? grid, distribute the grid to students and ask them to complete the grid independently. A sample completed grid is shown on page 58.

7. When students have finished, review the words and ask students who marked an "x" in the *Know It Well* column to explain what they know about the words.

8. Finally, invite students to make predictions about the content of the lesson. After the lesson, the words can be revisited to assess knowledge gained about the words.

References

Blachowicz, C.L.Z. (1986). Making connections: Alternatives to the vocabulary notebook. *Journal of Reading, 29*, 643–649.

Blachowicz, C., & Fisher, P. (2001). *Teaching vocabulary in all classrooms* (2nd ed.). Upper Saddle River, NJ: Merrill Prentice Hall.

How Well Do I Know These Words?

DIRECTIONS Here are some words from your reading. Before you read, put an "x" in the box that tells how well you think you know each word.

Word	1 Know It Well	2 Think I Know It	3 Don't Know It
caribou	X		
reindeer	X		
tundra		X	
migrate		X	
lichen			X
graze		X	
marsh			X
mosquitoes	X		

From Jerry L. Johns, Susan Davis Lenski, and Roberta L. Berglund, *Comprehension and Vocabulary Strategies for the Primary Grades*. Copyright © 2003 by Kendall/Hunt Publishing Company (1-800-247-3458, ext. 4 or 5). May be reproduced for noncommercial educational purposes within the guidelines noted on the copyright page.

 # How Well Do I Know These Words?

DIRECTIONS Here are some words from your reading. Before you read, put an "x" in the box that tells how well you think you know each word.

Word	1 Know It Well	2 Think I Know It	3 Don't Know It

Based on Blachowicz, C.L.Z. (1986). Making connections: Alternatives to the vocabulary notebook. *Journal of Reading, 29,* 643–649 and Blachowicz, C., & Fisher, P. (2001). *Teaching vocabulary in all classrooms* (2nd ed.). Upper Saddle River, NJ: Merrill Prentice Hall.

From Jerry L. Johns, Susan Davis Lenski, and Roberta L. Berglund, *Comprehension and Vocabulary Strategies for the Primary Grades.* Copyright © 2003 by Kendall/Hunt Publishing Company (1-800-247-3458, ext. 4 or 5). May be reproduced for noncommercial educational purposes within the guidelines noted on the copyright page.

LIST-GROUP-LABEL

FOCUS		TEXT		WHEN			WHY									HOW			
Comprehension	Vocabulary	Narrative	Informational	Before Reading	During Reading	After Reading	Predicting	Connecting	Questioning	Using Text Structure	Visualizing	Inferring	Summarizing	Synthesizing	Determining Importance	Individual	Partner	Small Group	Whole Group
●	●		●			●		●							●			●	

Description

List-Group-Label (Taba, 1967) helps students to organize information in categorical form. By classifying and categorizing information, students become active readers and, in the process, remember new vocabulary and information.

Procedure

1. Introduce a major concept or topic to students and invite them to share ideas, words, phrases, and/or experiences related to the topic. For example, *pioneers* is a topic often studied in the primary grades.

2. As students share their words and ideas, list words related to the topic on the board or an overhead transparency. For example, words related to *pioneers* might be *covered wagon, Native Americans, buckskin, hardships*, and *frontier.* Try to keep the number of responses to 20 or 25 for ease of management.

3. When the brainstormed words have been listed, read them aloud to the students. Ask students if there are ways that they think some of the words might be clustered together into categories or groups that are connected in some way. List these categories on the board or overhead transparency.

4. Put students into small groups and assign each group one of the categories. Give students a copy of the reproducible master on page 63. Ask students to choose words related to their category from the list on the board or overhead transparency. Ask them to think about how the words are connected to the category. It is often possible for some of the brainstormed words to become category headings. When this happens, groups might work on more than one category or a new group might be formed to focus on the new category.

5. When students have finished selecting the words they believe fit into their assigned category, invite each group to orally share the words they have included on their list with the entire class. You may wish to record these on the board or on an overhead transparency created from the reproducible master on page 63 or 64.

6. It is important for students to share reasons for their decisions. Words may be used in more than one category if the students' rationale supports such inclusion. This oral sharing stimulates students to think of the words in a variety of ways, consider their meanings, connect them, and see relationships among the words. A completed example for one group can be found on page 62.

7. If List-Group-Label is used as a prereading activity, ask students to then read or listen to the text and evaluate their decisions as they read or listen. Students may want to think about adding or deleting some words from their category list based on additional information in the lesson.

8. If List-Group-Label is used as a postreading activity, students may want to return to the groups and confirm their reasons for and accuracy of the words they included on the list for their category. They may also wish to use their completed lists to help them review and remember information in the lesson.

9. The List-Group-Label procedure can be extended over the course of several days as students acquire additional information about the topic. More words can be added to the categorized lists as students expand their knowledge and increase the connections they make between and among the words.

10. When the lists are complete, have students work individually or in pairs to write a summary of the information in one of the clusters or write a longer piece about the topic, using each one of the clusters of information as a paragraph in the longer piece.

Reference

Taba, H. (1967). *Teacher's handbook for elementary social studies.* Reading, MA: Addison-Wesley.

List-Group-Label

DIRECTIONS Write the names of the children in your group on the lines below. Then write the name of what you are studying and your group's category on the lines below your names. Next, look at the list of words. Choose the words that fit your category and write them under the column Our Words. Talk with other people in your group. Decide why each word should be in your category. Write your reason for choosing each word on the line next to the word.

Members of Our Group

Keeyan	Nigel	Dinah	Nicole

Pioneers

What We Are Studying

What They Ate

Our Group's Category

Our Words	Why We Think They Fit in This Category
buffalo	They lived on the prairie and they hunted them.
rabbits	Rabbits can be used for food.
corn	We think they grew corn on their farms.
vegetables	The pioneer wives worked in gardens.
chickens	They brought chickens with them in the wagons.

Name _____ Date _____

List-Group-Label

DIRECTIONS Write the names of the children in your group on the lines below. Then write the name of what you are studying and your group's category on the lines below your names. Next, look at the list of words. Choose the words that fit your category and write them under the column, Our Words. Talk with other people in your group. Decide why each word should be in your category. Write your reason for choosing each word on the line next to the word.

Members of Our Group

_____

_____

What We Are Studying

_____

Our Group's Category

_____

Our Words	Why We Think They Fit in This Category
_____	_____
_____	_____
_____	_____
_____	_____
_____	_____

From Jerry L. Johns, Susan Davis Lenski, and Roberta L. Berglund, *Comprehension and Vocabulary Strategies for the Primary Grades*. Copyright © 2003 by Kendall/Hunt Publishing Company (1-800-247-3458, ext. 4 or 5). May be reproduced for noncommercial educational purposes within the guidelines noted on the copyright page.

Name _____ Date _____

 # List-Group-Label

Topic
_____

Category   Category

_____   _____

Words   Words

_____   _____

_____   _____

_____   _____

_____   _____

_____   _____

_____   _____

_____   _____

_____   _____

_____   _____

From Jerry L. Johns, Susan Davis Lenski, and Roberta L. Berglund, *Comprehension and Vocabulary Strategies for the Primary Grades*. Copyright © 2003 by Kendall/Hunt Publishing Company (1-800-247-3458, ext. 4 or 5). May be reproduced for noncommercial educational purposes within the guidelines noted on the copyright page.

MYSTERY WORD BUBBLES

FOCUS		TEXT		WHEN			WHY									HOW			
Comprehension	Vocabulary	Narrative	Informational	Before Reading	During Reading	After Reading	Predicting	Connecting	Questioning	Using Text Structure	Visualizing	Inferring	Summarizing	Synthesizing	Determining Importance	Individual	Partner	Small Group	Whole Group
	●		●			●		●						●		●			

Description

Mystery Word Bubbles (Richardson & Morgan, 2002) are similar to Semantic Maps (see page 108) and Concept Circles (see page 25) and can be used as a scaffolding experience to lead students into these related strategies. Mystery Word Bubbles should be used as a postreading activity for review and to reinforce key concepts.

Procedure

1. Select the key concept words that you wish students to know. Draw an oval shape with three lines drawn vertically from the oval for each concept word or use the reproducible master on page 69. You may also wish to make an overhead transparency of How to Solve Mystery Word Bubbles on page 68.

2. Place one clue word or phrase related to each key concept word on one of the three legs extending downward from its oval. For younger or less able students, you may wish to place word or phrase clues on more than one of the legs.

3. Provide students with a list of vocabulary words, including the key concept words, selected from the unit of study. For example, in studying the solar system, choose words that name some of the planets, as well as characteristics unique to the individual planets. Refer to the example on page 67.

4. Invite students to use the clue words or phrases from the legs below the ovals to solve the mystery concept word that should go in each oval. You might say the following.

> We have been studying our solar system. To help us review what we have learned, I have created some mysteries for you to solve. I have given you some clues, and now you need to be good detectives. Remember to think about what you know about the planets in our solar system and see if you can use my clues and your good detective skills to figure out the mystery words.

Let's do one together. The first Mystery Word Bubble has the word *largest* written as a clue below it. Does anyone remember what the largest planet is?" [Elicit the correct response, *Jupiter*.]

You have solved the first part of the mystery by correctly identifying Jupiter as the largest planet in our solar system. Now let's solve the rest of the mystery by figuring out which of the remaining clues will tell us more about Jupiter. [Continue working with students until they have added *made of gas* and *red spot*.]

5. Students should use additional clues and phrases to help them solve the remaining Mystery Word Bubbles.

6. As students become more proficient with this strategy, you may wish to eliminate the use of a word list and have students use their textbooks and other reference sources to solve the word mysteries. You may also wish to provide them with copies of the reproducible master How to Solve Mystery Word Bubbles on page 68.

7. Students enjoy making Mystery Word Bubbles for others to solve. Their work can be reproduced and placed in one of the classroom's learning centers for use in independent or small group work.

Reference

Richardson, J.S., & Morgan, R.F. (2002). *Reading to learn in the content areas* (5th ed.). Belmont, CA: Wadsworth.

Mystery Word Bubbles

DIRECTIONS Solve the following word mysteries.

Planets
_____
Topic

Word Clues

- largest planet
- Earth
- has water
- red spot

- second planet from sun
- oxygen
- Mercury
- closest to the sun

- hottest planet
- Jupiter
- Earth's twin
- living things

- made of gas
- Venus
- smallest
- bright

Mystery Word Bubbles

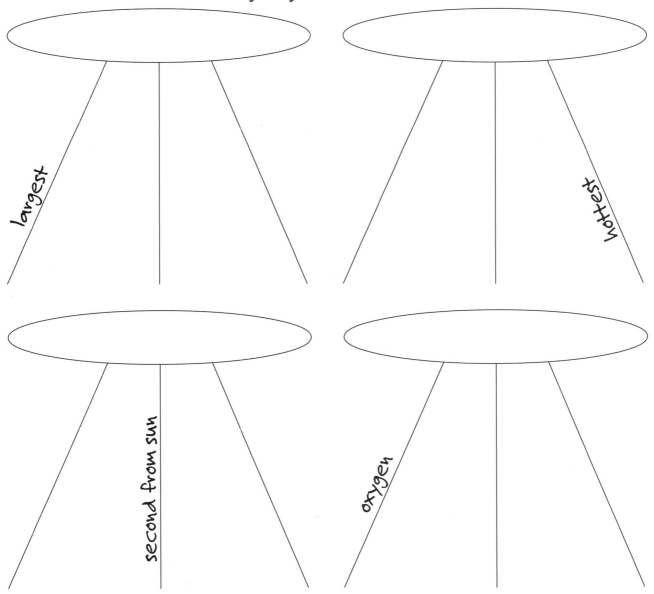

How to Solve
Mystery Word Bubbles

Can you be a word detective and use the clues to solve the word mysteries?

1. Look at the word or phrase on the line below one of the bubbles.

2. Now look at the list of words. What big idea does the clue word below the bubble make you think of?

3. When you think you know the bubble word, write that word inside the bubble.

4. Now look at the word list again. Are there other words that go with the one you have written inside the bubble?

5. Write those words on the lines below the bubble. You have solved one of the mysteries!

6. Now see if you can solve the remaining word mysteries.

From Jerry L. Johns, Susan Davis Lenski, and Roberta L. Berglund, *Comprehension and Vocabulary Strategies for the Primary Grades*. Copyright © 2003 by Kendall/Hunt Publishing Company (1-800-247-3458, ext. 4 or 5). May be reproduced for noncommercial educational purposes within the guidelines noted on the copyright page.

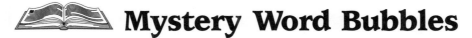

Mystery Word Bubbles

DIRECTIONS Solve the following word mysteries.

_____

Topic

Word Clues

_____ _____ _____

_____ _____ _____

_____ _____ _____

_____ _____ _____

Mystery Word Bubbles

From Jerry L. Johns, Susan Davis Lenski, and Roberta L. Berglund, *Comprehension and Vocabulary Strategies for the Primary Grades*. Copyright © 2003 by Kendall/Hunt Publishing Company (1-800-247-3458, ext. 4 or 5). May be reproduced for noncommercial educational purposes within the guidelines noted on the copyright page. 69

PAIRED QUESTIONING

FOCUS		TEXT		WHEN			WHY									HOW			
Comprehension	Vocabulary	Narrative	Informational	Before Reading	During Reading	After Reading	Predicting	Connecting	Questioning	Using Text Structure	Visualizing	Inferring	Summarizing	Synthesizing	Determining Importance	Individual	Partner	Small Group	Whole Group
●		●	●		●	●	●	●	●			●					●		

Description

Paired Questioning (McLaughlin & Allen, 2002; Vaughan & Estes, 1986) involves putting students in pairs, having them read short segments of narrative or informational text, and then questioning each other about its content. Paired Questioning is an adaptation of the ReQuest procedure developed by Manzo (1969). Paired Questioning gives students practice in developing questions on a variety of levels and helps students learn to select and defend their choices regarding the main ideas and important details in a text.

Procedure

1. Divide the class into pairs of students.

2. Share the guidelines of the Paired Questioning procedure (see page 72) with students and explain it as needed.

3. When students understand the guidelines, invite students to begin by reading the title or chapter heading of the text. You might model the procedure by reading aloud to the class the title from the book, *How Animals Move* (Byrne, 1998).

4. Next, put the book aside and invite students to ask you a question about the book. You might hold up the book and say the following.

    Mrs. Shafer: I just read the title of this book aloud to you. Can one of you ask me a question about the book?

    Jasper: What do you think this book will be about?

    Mrs. Shafer: I think this book might help me learn more about how different kinds of animals move. I did the best I could to answer your question. Now, without showing you the book again, I am going to ask you a question about the book. Why is movement important to an animal's survival?

This is an important opportunity to model a question involving an inference or one that engenders higher-level thinking.

5.   After a student has answered your question, repeat the modeling with a short segment of text or the contents page, if appropriate.

6.   Continue to model the Paired Questioning procedure until you believe that students understand it. Then refer students again to the Paired Questioning procedure (see page 72) and have them continue reading and posing questions with their partners.

7.   In order to continue modeling good questioning techniques, you may wish to use the strategy when reading aloud to students in small and large group settings.

8.   As an alternative to Paired Questioning, you may want to have students use the Say Something strategy (Short, Harste, & Burke, 1996) at the stopping points in the text instead of asking and answering questions.

References

Byrne, D. (1998). *How animals move*. Barrington, IL: Rigby.

Manzo, A.V. (1969). ReQuest procedure. *Journal of Reading, 13*, 123–126.

McLaughlin, M., & Allen, M.B. (2002). *Guided comprehension: A teaching model for grades 3–8*. Newark, DE: International Reading Association.

Short, K.G., Harste, J.C., & Burke, C. (1996). *Creating classrooms for authors and inquirers*. Portsmouth, NH: Heinemann.

Vaughan, J.L., & Estes, T.H. (1986). *Reading and reasoning beyond the primary grades*. Boston: Allyn and Bacon.

Paired Questioning

What To Do

1. Find a quiet place to work with your partner.

2. If you are sharing a book, sit so you and your partner can both see the words and illustrations clearly.

3. Begin by silently reading the title or heading.

4. Close the book or turn it over. Think of a question to ask your partner. After your partner answers it, have your partner ask you a question. Be sure you and your partner agree on the answers.

5. Now read the next section of the text silently. Think of one or more questions you might ask your partner about this section.

6. When you both finish reading, close the book again. Take turns asking each other questions and answering them. Remember to do the best you can to answer your partner's questions.

7. When you finish all of your reading, decide what you think are the most important ideas. Be ready to tell why you think so.

8. Tell your ideas to your partner. Your partner should tell you if she or he agrees with your ideas.

9. Finally, your partner should tell you his or her most important ideas and why. Decide if you agree or disagree.

10. If there is still time left, you and your partner should draw a picture showing the most important ideas from your reading. You might also write a short summary of your reading to share with the rest of the class.

From Jerry L. Johns, Susan Davis Lenski, and Roberta L. Berglund, *Comprehension and Vocabulary Strategies for the Primary Grades*. Copyright © 2003 by Kendall/Hunt Publishing Company (1-800-247-3458, ext. 4 or 5). May be reproduced for noncommercial educational purposes within the guidelines noted on the copyright page.

PICTURE SORT

FOCUS		TEXT		WHEN			WHY									HOW			
Comprehension	Vocabulary	Narrative	Informational	Before Reading	During Reading	After Reading	Predicting	Connecting	Questioning	Using Text Structure	Visualizing	Inferring	Summarizing	Synthesizing	Determining Importance	Individual	Partner	Small Group	Whole Group
●		●		●	●	●	●			●						●	●	●	●

Description

A Picture Sort engages students in an activity where they arrange pictures in an order that is similar to a story. This strategy can be used before, during, and after reading. It helps students make predictions about the story, revise their predictions, and, after reading, to retell and/or rewrite the story.

Procedure

1. Select a story with a clear plot that can be told by pictures.

2. Duplicate the sample Picture Sort cards. Draw a few pictures from a book using one picture per card or draw pictures based on a story you make up. Duplicate the cards for each student and have students separate the cards by cutting.

3. Tell students that you would like them to arrange the pictures in a certain order. If you're using Picture Sorts before reading, ask students to arrange the pictures in the order they think the story will be told. An example using the book *Stand Tall, Molly Lou Melon* (Lovell, 2001) follows.

    I will be reading a book to you today titled *Stand Tall, Molly Lou Melon*. The book was written by Patty Lovell and it was illustrated by David Catrow. Let's look at the front cover and make predictions about the story.

    Today, I'm going to have you make additional predictions. Before you read the book, I'd like you to make predictions by using these picture cards. The pictures are events in the story. Arrange the pictures as you think the story will occur.

4. You can also use the Picture Sort cards during reading. If you're using them during reading, have students organize the pictures to show the events in the story while you read. An example of what you could say follows.

You have all made predictions about the story using your Picture Sort cards. Now I will read the story. If you hear something different from your predictions, change the order of your cards.

5. Picture Sort cards are also useful as an after-reading strategy. If you're using Picture Sorts after reading, have students check to see whether they arranged the pictures in the order of the story and to retell the story to a friend using the Picture Sort cards.

6. An example of Picture Sort cards using the story *Stand Tall, Molly Lou Melon* (Lovell, 2001) is on page 75, and a reproducible master of Picture Sort cards follows on page 76.

Reference

Lovell, P. (2001). *Stand tall, Molly Lou Melon*. New York: G.P. Putnam's Sons.

Picture Sort

Stand Tall, Molly Lou Melon by P. Lovell

 **Picture Sort**

Title and Author

From Jerry L. Johns, Susan Davis Lenski, and Roberta L. Berglund, *Comprehension and Vocabulary Strategies for the Primary Grades*. Copyright © 2003 by Kendall/Hunt Publishing Company (1-800-247-3458, ext. 4 or 5). May be reproduced for noncommercial educational purposes within the guidelines noted on the copyright page.

PLUS, MINUS, INTERESTING (PMI)

FOCUS		TEXT		WHEN			WHY									HOW			
Comprehension	Vocabulary	Narrative	Informational	Before Reading	During Reading	After Reading	Predicting	Connecting	Questioning	Using Text Structure	Visualizing	Inferring	Summarizing	Synthesizing	Determining Importance	Individual	Partner	Small Group	Whole Group
●		●	●			●		●				●				●	●	●	●

Description

Plus, Minus, Interesting (PMI), (deBono, 1976; Fogarty & Bellanca, 1991), involves students in constructing meaning from and responding to a text after reading. This reflective activity invites students to analyze text for its positive, negative, and interesting features, as well as for information and/or impact. PMI encourages students to make connections with and formulate opinions about material they have listened to or read.

Procedure

1. Make a transparency using the reproducible master on page 80 or draw a PMI organizer on the board. Create columns for P (Plus), M (Minus), and I (Interesting).

2. Read a portion of a text (either narrative or informational) aloud to students. For example, a story that could be read aloud to primary students might be *The Velveteen Rabbit* (Williams, 1958).

3. Following the reading, record something you liked about the text. In the case of informational text, record something that is potentially good or beneficial about the information. Put your ideas under the column labeled P for Plus. An example of a positive comment that might be written about *The Velveteen Rabbit* could be, "It made me feel happy when the boy took the rabbit that he loved so much with him wherever he went."

4. Invite students to offer additional ideas for the Plus column based on their reactions to the text. You might ask, "Was there something in the book that made you feel happy or something that you thought was especially good about the story?" Then list students' ideas in the Plus column.

5. Now move to the Minus (M) column. Here you should list something you did not like about the text. In the case of informational text, list some bad or negative impact the information discussed may have had. For example, a minus for *The Velveteen Rabbit* might be, "I felt sorry for the Velveteen Rabbit when the real rabbits made fun of him. Teasing hurts." Once you have offered an idea or two, invite students to suggest additional thoughts for the M column and record them.

6. The final column is the Interesting (I) column. Now it is your turn to record something interesting about what was read. For example, you might say, "To me it was interesting that children sometimes think their special toys are real." Students then have a turn to add the ideas that they found interesting to the I column on the chart.

7. After this strategy has been modeled with one type of text, provide copies of the reproducible master on page 80 for students to use as they read a text of the same genre independently or with a partner.

8. When students have completed the reading and their PMI sheets, they should use them in a small or large group discussion. Students then have an opportunity to share their ideas with others and listen to the comments generated by other group members.

References

deBono, E. (1976). *Teaching thinking*. New York: Penguin Books.

Fogarty, R., & Bellanca, J. (1991). *Patterns for thinking, patterns for transfer*. Palatine, IL: Skylight.

Williams, M. (1958). *The velveteen rabbit*. New York: Doubleday.

The Velveteen Rabbit

Title

Plus +	Minus −	Interesting
It made me feel happy when the boy took the rabbit that he loved so much with him wherever he went.	I felt sorry for the Velveteen Rabbit when the real rabbits made fun of him. Teasing hurts.	It was interesting that children sometimes think their special toys are real.

Title

Plus +	Minus ~	Interesting

From Jerry L. Johns, Susan Davis Lenski, and Roberta L. Berglund, *Comprehension and Vocabulary Strategies for the Primary Grades*. Copyright © 2003 by Kendall/Hunt Publishing Company (1-800-247-3458, ext. 4 or 5). May be reproduced for noncommercial educational purposes within the guidelines noted on the copyright page.

POSSIBLE SENTENCES

FOCUS		TEXT		WHEN			WHY									HOW			
Comprehension	Vocabulary	Narrative	Informational	Before Reading	During Reading	After Reading	Predicting	Connecting	Questioning	Using Text Structure	Visualizing	Inferring	Summarizing	Synthesizing	Determining Importance	Individual	Partner	Small Group	Whole Group
●	●		●	●	●	●	●	●				●				●	●		●

Description

Possible Sentences (Moore & Moore, 1992) is a strategy that will help students predict the content of a selection. They then check their predictions while reading or listening. After reading, students use the text to support the accuracy of their sentences or revise them so they become more reflective of the content. The Possible Sentences strategy helps students set a purpose for reading or listening and develops an interest in and curiosity about the text.

Procedure

1. Identify 6–10 key vocabulary words (some new, some familiar) from a selected text. Write them on the board, overhead transparency, or reproducible master and pronounce the words for the students.

2. Model using two of the words in a single sentence. Write the sentence on the board or overhead transparency. Underline the vocabulary words in the sentence. For example, the following words are from *You Can Measure* (Mansk, 2003): ruler, measuring tape, scale, plant, kitten, measuring cup, and food. You might say the following.

    > Let's see if I can make a sentence using the words *scale* and *kitten*. Perhaps the book will say, "The *kitten* was weighed on the *scale*." I could also make another sentence with *measuring tape* and *plant*. "I used a <u>measuring tape</u> to see how tall mom's <u>plant</u> was."

3. Continue writing sentences together with the students until all the vocabulary words are used.

4. Direct students to read the text selection or read it together as a class.

5. After reading the selection, reread each Possible Sentence with students to determine its accuracy. For beginning readers, you may want to use a **star** for true, a **sad face** for an inaccurate prediction, and a **question mark** for those you aren't sure of because adequate information is not available. For students in grades two and above, a **T** can be used for true, an **F** for false, and **DK** for don't know. Encourage students to cite specific text references to support their conclusions about the accuracy of the sentences.

6. You may choose to correct the statements that are inaccurate. Students in grades two and above could do research for further information for the don't know statements.

7. When the activity is repeated, students (if they are writing), can do the activity using the reproducible master on page 83 or page 84.

References

Mansk, A. (2003). *You can measure*. New York: Sadlier-Oxford.

Moore, D.W., Moore, S.A. (1992). Posssible sentences: An update. In E.K. Dishner, T.W. Bean, J.E. Readence, & D.W. Moore (Eds.), *Reading in the content areas* (3rd ed.) (pp. 196–202). Dubuque, IA: Kendall/Hunt.

 # Possible Sentences

_____

Title of Selection

Below are some words you will find in your reading.

_____   _____

_____   _____

_____   _____

_____   _____

_____   _____

Possible Sentences

[DIRECTIONS] Write one or more sentences using at least two of the above words in each sentence. Underline the words you use from the list above. After reading, rate the sentences by using the following key:

★ = true   ☹ = false   **?** = don't know

_____ 1. _____

_____

_____ 2. _____

_____

_____ 3. _____

_____

_____ 4. _____

_____

From Jerry L. Johns, Susan Davis Lenski, and Roberta L. Berglund, *Comprehension and Vocabulary Strategies for the Primary Grades*. Copyright © 2003 by Kendall/Hunt Publishing Company (1-800-247-3458, ext. 4 or 5). May be reproduced for noncommercial educational purposes within the guidelines noted on the copyright page.

📖 Possible Sentences

_____

Title of Selection

Below are some words you will find in your reading.

_____   _____

_____   _____

_____   _____

_____   _____

_____   _____

Possible Sentences

DIRECTIONS Write one or more sentences using at least two of the above words in each sentence. Underline the words you use from the list above. After reading, rate the sentences by using the following key:

T = true   F = false   DK = don't know

_____ 1. _____

_____

_____ 2. _____

_____

_____ 3. _____

_____

_____ 4. _____

_____

From Jerry L. Johns, Susan Davis Lenski, and Roberta L. Berglund, *Comprehension and Vocabulary Strategies for the Primary Grades*. Copyright © 2003 by Kendall/Hunt Publishing Company (1-800-247-3458, ext. 4 or 5). May be reproduced for noncommercial educational purposes within the guidelines noted on the copyright page.

PREDICT-O-GRAM

FOCUS		TEXT		WHEN			WHY									HOW			
Comprehension	Vocabulary	Narrative	Informational	Before Reading	During Reading	After Reading	Predicting	Connecting	Questioning	Using Text Structure	Visualizing	Inferring	Summarizing	Synthesizing	Determining Importance	Individual	Partner	Small Group	Whole Group
●	●	●		●	●	●	●		●	●		●				●	●	●	●

Description

A Predict-O-Gram (Blachowicz, 1986) invites students to use their knowledge of story structure to assign words to categories prior to reading. Examples of the categories include setting, characters, and actions. The teacher selects the words to be categorized. Students can discuss reasons for their placement of words prior to reading. After reading, students can compare their predictions with the text and revise the Predict-O-Gram.

Procedure

1. Use items 1–3 if students do not understand basic story structure, and take time to help them acquire such knowledge. You might begin by telling a story and clearly stating the story elements and writing them on the board. Create your own story or use the example below.

   > Erica and Emily decided to practice kicking a soccer ball. They looked and looked all over the house, but they couldn't find the ball. They decided to ask their dad. Dad suggested that they look in the hall closet. Sure enough! The ball was tucked in the corner of the closet under a jacket that had fallen on it. The girls took the ball to the back yard and began to practice by kicking the ball.

2. Guide students to understand the basic story elements. You might say the following.

   > There are ways that all stories are alike. Stories have characters; they can be people or animals. Who are the characters in this story? Tell me and I'll write them under *characters*. [As students share, write the names of the characters.] Guide students as needed (e.g., Who else is mentioned in the story?) and address or clarify incorrect responses.

   > Stories also have a setting—that means they take place somewhere at some time. Where does this story take place? [Have students share and write words under the category *setting* or *place*.]

A story also has a problem or conflict. Who can tell me the problem? I'll write it under *problem* [Clarify as needed.] Finally, stories have a solution. Solution means how the problem is solved. What is the solution in our story? I'll write it on the board.

3. Highlight the basic story elements from your example and help students understand that all stories have these basic elements. Take time to develop an understanding of story structure using additional examples and/or by reading stories to the class. You may develop this understanding through multiple exposures to stories and through intentionally focused instruction. Consider using some of the following ideas.

    *   Oral stories that use your students' names and familiar locations
    *   Nursery rhymes
    *   Common stories such as *The Three Little Pigs*
    *   *Aunt Isabel Tells a Good One* (Duke, 1992)—an excellent, engaging introduction to story grammar for students

4. When you believe students possess a basic knowledge of story structure, introduce the Predict-O-Gram to the entire class or to a small group of students. Adapt the Predict-O-Gram to suit your students' needs. Help students connect their knowledge of story structure to the Predict-O-Gram by saying something like the following.

    As we've shared stories orally and through reading, you have learned that all stories have settings, characters, problems, and solutions. [Review as necessary.] Today we'll use our knowledge of stories to predict where certain words from the story might fit on this chart. [Highlight chart elements as needed.]

5. From a simple story that is unfamiliar to students, select several key words. List the words on the board, chart paper, overhead transparency, or on a reproduced copy of a Predict-O-Gram.

6. Use whole group or small group instruction the first time you introduce the Predict-O-Gram. You can gradually move to more independent work as students exhibit readiness and understanding.

7. Invite students to predict what will happen in the story by suggesting words from the list in the boxes of the Predict-O-Gram. As students share their predictions, write them in the chart. If necessary, read the words to the students. Encourage students to give reasons for their choices.

8. When all the words have been placed in the Predict-O-Gram, invite students to predict what the story might be about. The particular words you choose for the strategy can help determine the degree of difficulty. Then read the story to students or, if appropriate, have students read it independently.

9. After the story has been read, use the Predict-O-Gram to review the predictions as compared to the story. Words may be moved to the correct places on the Predict-O-Gram. Some teachers use a magnetic white board and word cards to make it easier to move words. Other teachers use chart paper and word cards with tape on the back so words can be moved.

10. Help students understand that this strategy can help them think about the parts or elements in all stories they read or hear. This knowledge of the elements will help them remember the story.

Predict-O-Gram

purple	wondered	break
Matthew	crayon	upstairs
sidewalk	Tilly	sorry

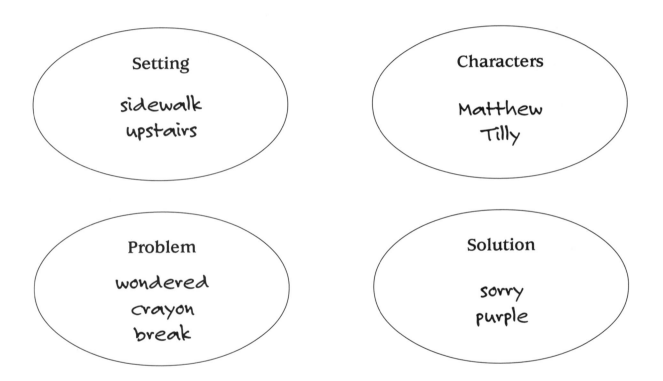

Setting

sidewalk
upstairs

Characters

Matthew
Tilly

Problem

wondered
crayon
break

Solution

sorry
purple

11. Two Predict-O-Gram reproducible masters can be found on pages 88–89. One is intended for early experiences with this strategy; the other can be used with older students and to expand the basic elements of a story. The Predict-O-Gram can also be used to help students structure their writing. Words for their stories can be placed in the Predict-O-Gram and then crossed out or checked off as they are used in the story.

References

Blachowicz, C.L.Z. (1986). Making connections: Alternatives to the vocabulary notebook. *Journal of Reading, 29,* 643–649.

Duke, K. (1992). *Aunt Isabel tells a good one*. New York: Puffin.

Name _____ Date _____

 Predict-O-Gram

DIRECTIONS Put the words where you think they fit best. Write them on the lines in the boxes.

_____ _____ _____

_____ _____ _____

_____ _____ _____

Place/Setting	
	_____ _____
	_____ _____
Characters	
	_____ _____
	_____ _____
Problem	
	_____ _____
	_____ _____
Solution	
	_____ _____
	_____ _____

From Jerry L. Johns, Susan Davis Lenski, and Roberta L. Berglund, *Comprehension and Vocabulary Strategies for the Primary Grades*. Copyright © 2003 by Kendall/Hunt Publishing Company (1-800-247-3458, ext. 4 or 5). May be reproduced for noncommercial educational purposes within the guidelines noted on the copyright page.

Name _____ Date _____

 **Predict-O-Gram**

_____

Title

DIRECTIONS How do you think these words will be used in the story? Write them in a square on the Predict-O-Gram. You may have more than one word in a square.

_____

_____

_____

_____

Setting	Characters	Goal or Problem
Events or Something That Happens	Solution	Other Things

Based on Blachowicz, C.L.Z. (1986). Making connections: Alternatives to the vocabulary notebook. *Journal of Reading*, *29*, 643–649.

From Jerry L. Johns, Susan Davis Lenski, and Roberta L. Berglund, *Comprehension and Vocabulary Strategies for the Primary Grades*. Copyright © 2003 by Kendall/Hunt Publishing Company (1-800-247-3458, ext. 4 or 5). May be reproduced for noncommercial educational purposes within the guidelines noted on the copyright page.

PREDICTION CHART

FOCUS		TEXT		WHEN			WHY									HOW			
Comprehension	Vocabulary	Narrative	Informational	Before Reading	During Reading	After Reading	Predicting	Connecting	Questioning	Using Text Structure	Visualizing	Inferring	Summarizing	Synthesizing	Determining Importance	Individual	Partner	Small Group	Whole Group
●		●	●	●	●		●		●							●	●	●	●

Description

A Prediction Chart is an organizational tool for students to use as they make and confirm predictions before and during reading. Before reading, students should make predictions based on the title, front cover, and illustrations of the story. As students read, they should continue to make and confirm their predictions to deepen their comprehension of the story. Teachers can use Prediction Charts during Shared Reading, and they can also encourage students to use them while reading independently. Most students will need to have the Prediction Chart demonstrated several times with different selections.

Procedure

1. Tell students that they need to think about the title of a story before they begin reading. Explain that when they think about the story before reading, they are getting their minds ready to read. You might use a computer analogy with some students similar to the example below.

   I'm going to read a new book titled *Wolf!* (Bloom, 1999). When I read the title, I boot up my computer files on the things I know about wolves. In my mind, I have all sorts of information about wolves, stories about wolves, and the time I saw a wolf in Alaska. All of this information is in my mind, much like a folder in a computer titled *wolves*. I open that folder and think about all of the things I know about wolves before I begin reading the story.

2. Remind students that as they think about the title of a story, they should also look at the picture on the cover. The picture often clues readers into the kind of story it will be. For example, you might say something like the following.

   As I look at the cover of the book *Wolf!*, I notice several things. First, I notice that the title ends with an exclamation point. I've never seen a title with that type of punctuation, and I'm not sure what it means, but I think it will be a different type of wolf story. Then I look at the picture on the cover, and I find that the picture is not realistic—the animals are drawn like cartoon characters. The wolf has on a pair of glasses, and he's reading a book with a pig and a cow. A duck is looking over his shoulder.

The picture on the cover tells me a number of things. First, I don't think the story will be real but will be made up. Second, it looks like it will be a funny story. It also will probably be something about reading because there are books on the cover and a wolf is reading.

3. Have students practice predicting by using the title and cover picture from several other books. Remind students that predicting before reading is an important part of reading comprehension.

4. At another session, draw a Prediction Chart on the board or on chart paper, or, if you have students who can read and write independently, copy the reproducible master of the Prediction Chart from page 93 and distribute it to students.

5. Remind students that they already learned that they should make predictions by using the title and picture on the cover for clues. Then tell students that they should also make predictions while they are reading.

6. Demonstrate the use of predictions while reading, as in the following example.

   After I read the first two pages of *Wolf!*, I stopped reading and thought about what had happened. At the beginning of the story, a hungry wolf stopped at a farm to look at the animals. The animals were reading.

   After I read these two pages, I predicted that the wolf would charge into the barnyard and grab the duck. I thought this because in many fairy tales the wolf tries to eat small animals.

7. Tell students that they can record their predictions on a Prediction Chart so that they remember what they thought. Point out the first predictions in the second column of the sample Prediction Chart under the heading, "What I am thinking about. . . ." Encourage students to make multiple predictions in this column.

8. Read several more pages of the book or have students read independently. Stop after a few pages and ask students to respond to the prompt, "Was I right? Why or why not?" Explain that many predictions are partially right and that, as they read, students should "confirm" their predictions by determining how close they were to the actual story. Show students the third column on the Prediction Chart that details how "right" the predictions were. Encourage students to use their knowledge of the story in their responses.

9. Use the Prediction Chart often, during read alouds, Shared Reading, guided reading, and independent reading. Model your own predictions and also elicit students' predictions. Encourage students to use a Prediction Chart as they read in pairs or independently.

10. A reproducible master of a Prediction Chart can be found on page 93.

Reference

Bloom, B. (1999). *Wolf!* New York: Orchard Books.

Prediction Chart

for _____ Wolf! by B. Bloom _____

Part of book	What I am thinking about . . .	Was I right? Why or why not?
Title and cover	Red Riding Hood Wolf in Alaska My cousin owns a wolf, and he's shy.	This story will be different than other wolf stories I've read. It looks like it will be funny.
First two pages	The wolf would charge the animals and grab the duck. The wolf would ask the animals for food. The wolf would eat the animal's supper.	The wolf did run out and try to scare the animals, but he didn't grab the duck. The wolf didn't ask the animals for food, but he howled. The wolf seemed to forget he was hungry because he was so surprised that the animals weren't scared.

Name _____ Date _____

 **Prediction Chart**

for _____

Part of book	What I am thinking about . . .	Was I right? Why or why not?

From Jerry L. Johns, Susan Davis Lenski, and Roberta L. Berglund, *Comprehension and Vocabulary Strategies for the Primary Grades*. Copyright © 2003 by Kendall/Hunt Publishing Company (1-800-247-3458, ext. 4 or 5). May be reproduced for noncommercial educational purposes within the guidelines noted on the copyright page.

QUESTIONING THE AUTHOR

FOCUS		TEXT		WHEN			WHY									HOW			
Comprehension	Vocabulary	Narrative	Informational	Before Reading	During Reading	After Reading	Predicting	Connecting	Questioning	Using Text Structure	Visualizing	Inferring	Summarizing	Synthesizing	Determining Importance	Individual	Partner	Small Group	Whole Group
●		●	●		●				●			●	●			●	●	●	●

Description

As students read, they need to be actively engaged in thinking about the meanings of the text. Students often read books, especially informational passages, without asking themselves the questions that would facilitate comprehension. A strategy that promotes comprehension through questioning during reading is Questioning the Author (Beck, McKeown, Hamilton, & Kucan, 1997). The idea behind Questioning the Author is that once students identify authors as real people who are trying to present a message, they can actively question the authors' intentions about the message of the text. Questioning the Author will take several demonstration sessions before most students begin applying this strategy consistently while they read.

Procedure

1. Hold up a book that you want students to read and tell students that one or more authors wrote the book. Explain to students that authors do the best job they can to express their ideas, but that sometimes authors are not very clear and that readers need to ask questions while they read. An example using the book *Pole to Pole* (Taylor, 1999) follows.

    Today we're going to read a book titled *Pole to Pole*. What do you think this book will be about? [Give students time to respond before answering. The book is about the North and South Poles.]

    What picture clues do we have that can help us predict what will be in the book? [The front cover has a picture of a wolf and a smaller picture of an ice house.]

    The author of this book is Barbara Taylor. She wrote this book to try to explain what it's like on the North and South Poles. She wrote this book for readers who had never visited either of the Poles so that we could know what it's like.

Barbara Taylor wrote this book for children, but adults like the book too. She wanted children to understand some facts about the Poles through this book.

2. Tell students that as they read *Pole to Pole* they should determine what Barbara Taylor was trying to communicate by asking questions as if she were right next to them. Explain to students that by asking questions of the author during reading, they will develop a better understanding of the book.

3. Duplicate and distribute the reproducible master of Questioning the Author on page 97. Tell students that they should ask themselves the questions on this sheet as they read.

4. Demonstrate how you would use the Questioning the Author sheet with a book of your choosing or use the example that follows.

    As I read from *Pole to Pole*, I was interested in the way the author organized the print. The pages are organized like a website or an encyclopedia. The organization made the book easier for me to read.

    One of the sections of the book that I liked best was on pages 10 and 11, Arctic Animals. I'll ask myself the questions using that part. Since there is only one author, I'll question the author rather than authors.

    The first question is, "What is the author trying to say here?" I think Barbara Taylor is trying to explain about the different animals in the arctic. She has paragraphs on seals, the arctic fritillary butterfly, walruses, auks, lemmings, and wolves.

    "Why did the author include these passages?" I think she wanted her readers to know a little bit about a few of the animals found at the North Pole. She lists some of the other birds and animals that live at the North Pole, one of which is a musk ox. I wish she had written about that animal.

    "Does the author explain things clearly?" Yes, she writes very clearly.

    "Is the author good at writing for children?" The book might have too many details for some children, but the illustrations make the book easy to read.

    "What could the author have done to make the book easier to understand?" Some of the sentences are pretty long and hard to follow. Shorter sentences might help.

    "In what ways is the author effective?" Barbara Taylor was able to get me to read all about the North and South Poles and to remember lots of information about both of them. The things she chose to write about were really interesting. She's a good writer.

5. Have students select a partner. Then ask students to read another section from the book you were modeling. Tell one student to pretend to be the author and the other one pretend to be the reader. Have students Question the Author through role playing.

6. After students have had several experiences role playing Questioning the Author, encourage students to ask the questions independently. They might ask the questions silently or they could write answers to questions on the accompanying reproducible master on page 97.

7. Remind students to ask questions frequently while they read.

References

Beck, I.L., McKeown, M.G., Hamilton, R.L., & Kucan, L. (1997). *Questioning the author: An approach for enhancing student engagement with text*. Newark, DE: International Reading Association.

Taylor, B. (1999). *Pole to pole*. Hauppauge, NY: Barron's.

Name _____ Date _____

Questioning the Author

1. What is the author trying to say here? _____

   _____

   _____

   _____

2. Why did the author include this passage or example? _____

   _____

   _____

3. Did the author explain things clearly? _____

   _____

   _____

4. Is the author good at writing for children? Why or why not? _____

   _____

   _____

5. What could the author have done to make this easier to understand? _____

   _____

   _____

6. In what ways did the author do a good job? _____

   _____

   _____

   _____

From Jerry L. Johns, Susan Davis Lenski, and Roberta L. Berglund, *Comprehension and Vocabulary Strategies for the Primary Grades*. Copyright © 2003 by Kendall/Hunt Publishing Company (1-800-247-3458, ext. 4 or 5). May be reproduced for noncommercial educational purposes within the guidelines noted on the copyright page.

RIVET

FOCUS		TEXT		WHEN			WHY									HOW			
Comprehension	Vocabulary	Narrative	Informational	Before Reading	During Reading	After Reading	Predicting	Connecting	Questioning	Using Text Structure	Visualizing	Inferring	Summarizing	Synthesizing	Determining Importance	Individual	Partner	Small Group	Whole Group
	●	●	●	●			●												●

Description

The primary goal of teaching vocabulary strategies is for students to increase comprehension, but many students do not stay actively involved in learning during traditional vocabulary lessons. To combat inattention during vocabulary lessons, Cunningham (2000) developed the strategy RIVET. During RIVET, teachers focus students' attention on the individual letters of the new words, and students become "riveted" on the words. Using RIVET also encourages the use of prior knowledge and predictions, which also fosters improved comprehension. "Activating children's prior knowledge and getting them to make predictions before they read is one sure way to increase the involvement and comprehension of most children" (Cunningham, 2000, p. 148).

Procedure

1. Identify a text that has new vocabulary terms that you would like students to be able to read. Read the text and select six to eight key words, with an emphasis on polysyllabic words and important names. For example, a list for a social studies book might include the following words.

    1. Americans
    2. Holidays
    3. Celebrate
    4. Thanksgiving
    5. Washington
    6. Presidents
    7. Memorial
    8. Independence

2. Write numbers for the list of words on the board with blanks for each letter of the words. For example, if your first word is *Americans*, write number one followed by nine blanks.

    1. __ __ __ __ __ __ __ __ __

3. Duplicate and distribute copies of the RIVET reproducible master on page 101.

4. Fill in the letters to the first word one at a time. Tell students to write the letters as you do and encourage them to predict the word as soon as they think they know it. For example, you might say the following.

> I've selected some words from our reading today that I want you to guess. The first word has nine blanks, so it has nine letters. I'm going to write one letter at a time and ask you to predict the word. I'll stop after each letter so you can make your guesses. Please raise your hands, and I'll call on one of you as soon as your hand is up.

5. As you fill in the letters, allow ample time for guessing the word. Once a student guesses the correct word, have him or her help you finish spelling it on the board while students write it on their papers. If students guess incorrect words, just continue writing letters until someone guesses the correct word. An example follows.

> 1. A m e r __ __ __ __ __

6. Continue writing the letters of each word until all words have been guessed and written correctly on the board and on the students' papers.

7. After students have completed their list of words, ask students to make predictions about the text. Encourage as many divergent predictions as possible by asking questions leading to alternative possibilities. For example, a student might say, "Americans are people who live in the United States." A leading question following that prediction could be, "Do all Americans live in the United States?" Continue asking for predictions for each of the words.

8. During discussions, students will learn the context of the vocabulary words. To deepen students' understandings of the words, ask them to predict a definition. Discuss possible definitions for words guiding students to develop an accurate meaning for the word, as in the example of a conversation about the word *Americans* that follows.

> Brad: Americans are people who live in the United States.
>
> Miss Wilcox: Do all Americans live in the United States?
>
> Samantha: There are other countries in America.
>
> Miss Wilcox: What other countries can you think of?
>
> José: Mexico and Canada are in North America.
>
> Miss Wilcox: Yes, they are. Is there another America?
>
> Maria: There's also Central America and South America.
>
> Miss Wilcox: Good. Can you now tell me a definition for Americans?

George: Americans are people who live in North, Central, and South America.

Miss Wilcox: Let's write that definition at the bottom of our RIVET sheet. That definition will help you as you read the social studies book today.

9. Instruct students to write the agreed upon definition at the bottom of the RIVET reproducible master on page 101.

Reference

Cunningham, P.M. (2000). *Phonics they use* (3rd ed). New York: Longman.

Name _____ Date _____

 # RIVET

DIRECTIONS Write the letters for the vocabulary words on the blanks with one letter for each blank. You might have some blanks left over. After class discussion, write what you think the words mean on the lines at the bottom of the page.

Vocabulary Words

1. __ __ __ __ __ __ __ __ __ __ __ __ __ __

2. __ __ __ __ __ __ __ __ __ __ __ __

3. __ __ __ __ __ __ __ __ __ __ __

4. __ __ __ __ __ __ __ __ __ __ __ __

5. __ __ __ __ __ __ __ __ __ __ __

6. __ __ __ __ __ __ __ __ __ __ __ __ __

7. __ __ __ __ __ __ __ __ __ __ __ __

8. __ __ __ __ __ __ __ __ __ __ __ __

What the Words Mean

1. _____

2. _____

3. _____

4. _____

5. _____

6. _____

7. _____

8. _____

Based on Cunningham, P.M. (2000). *Phonics they use* (3rd ed). New York: Longman.

From Jerry L. Johns, Susan Davis Lenski, and Roberta L. Berglund, *Comprehension and Vocabulary Strategies for the Primary Grades*. Copyright © 2003 by Kendall/Hunt Publishing Company (1-800-247-3458, ext. 4 or 5). May be reproduced for noncommercial educational purposes within the guidelines noted on the copyright page.

SEMANTIC FEATURE ANALYSIS

FOCUS		TEXT		WHEN			WHY									HOW			
Comprehension	Vocabulary	Narrative	Informational	Before Reading	During Reading	After Reading	Predicting	Connecting	Questioning	Using Text Structure	Visualizing	Inferring	Summarizing	Synthesizing	Determining Importance	Individual	Partner	Small Group	Whole Group
	●	●	●	●		●	●	●	●					●					●

Description

Semantic Feature Analysis (Johnson & Pearson, 1984; Pittelman, Heimlich, Berglund, & French, 1991) is an instructional strategy that helps students understand the uniqueness of a word, as well as its relationships to other words. It uses a grid system to help students determine semantic similarities and differences among words.

Procedure

1. Select a text about a topic for which your students have some background knowledge.

2. Write the name of the topic on a chart, the board, or an overhead transparency. List terms related to the topic down the left side of the grid. List features or properties related to the topic across the top of the grid. See the sample on page 104 and the reproducible master on page 105.

3. Discuss the first term and feature. Decide if the feature describes the term. If it does, put a plus (+) in the box. If it does not describe the term, put a minus (–) in the box. If students are unsure, then put a question mark (?) in the box. (A variation is to use smiley and sad faces.) You might say the following about *Look at these Animals* (Christopher, 2003).

> Miss Hett: Before I read this book about animals to you, I want you to share some things you know. Look at this chart with the names of some animals. I'll say the words. [Pronounce the words.] Now look at where it says, "can be pets." Let's put a plus (+) if the animal can be a pet, a minus (–) if it can't, and a question mark (?) if we aren't sure.

> Casey: I think a dog is a mammal, and it can be a pet.

> Miss Hett: Class, do you agree? Okay, what should we put here? [Point to where "dogs" and "can be pets" intersect.]

John: Put a plus. And you should also put a plus for birds, because I have a parakeet for a pet.

Kari: I have a fish for a pet so put a plus there.

Miss Hett: What about amphibians?

Corey: I think they are dangerous so they wouldn't be pets.

Miss Hett: I'll put a minus in that box. [See partially completed Semantic Feature Analysis Chart that follows. Complete the chart with teacher guidance, remembering that initial impressions may be incorrect.]

4. Have students read the selected text. Students might suggest any terms or features that can be added to the chart. They could also note any questions that are answered in the text.

5. Discuss the students' findings, adding appropriate information to the chart. After reading, students should discover that amphibians can also be pets, so the minus should be changed to a plus.

6. Complete additional Semantic Feature Analysis charts as a whole class activity. When students are familiar with the strategy, use or adapt the reproducible master on page 105. You may wish to use the term "Word Grid" in place of Semantic Feature Analysis.

References

Christopher, G. (2003). *Look at these animals*. New York: Sadlier-Oxford.

Johnson, D.D., & Pearson, P.D. (1984). *Teaching reading vocabulary* (2nd ed.). New York: Holt, Rinehart, and Winston.

Pittelman, S.D., Heimlich, J.E., Berglund, R.L., & French, M.P. (1991). *Semantic feature analysis: Classroom applications*. Newark, DE: International Reading Association.

Semantic Feature Analysis

Look at these Animals by G. Christopher

Words	Features								
	can be pets	cool, dry skin	hatch from eggs	wet, cool skin	scales	lay eggs	gills	wings	fur or hair
dogs	+	−	−	−	−				
birds	+	−	+	−	−				
fish	+	−	?	+	+				
amphibians	−	?	+	+	−				
reptiles	?	?	+	+	?				

Name _____ Date _____

 # Semantic Feature Analysis (SFA)

Features

Words

Based on Johnson, D.D., & Pearson, P.D. (1984). *Teaching reading vocabulary* (2nd ed.). New York: Holt, Rinehart, and Winston and Pittelman, S.D., Heimlich, J.E., Berglund, R.L., & French, M.P. (1991). *Semantic feature analysis: Classroom applications*. Newark, DE: International Reading Association.

From Jerry L. Johns, Susan Davis Lenski, and Roberta L. Berglund, *Comprehension and Vocabulary Strategies for the Primary Grades*. Copyright © 2003 by Kendall/Hunt Publishing Company (1-800-247-3458, ext. 4 or 5). May be reproduced for noncommercial educational purposes within the guidelines noted on the copyright page.

SEMANTIC MAPPING

FOCUS		TEXT		WHEN			WHY									HOW			
Comprehension	Vocabulary	Narrative	Informational	Before Reading	During Reading	After Reading	Predicting	Connecting	Questioning	Using Text Structure	Visualizing	Inferring	Summarizing	Synthesizing	Determining Importance	Individual	Partner	Small Group	Whole Group
●	●	●	●	●	●	●		●						●	●	●		●	

Description

Semantic Mapping (Heimlich & Pittelman, 1986; Johnson & Pearson, 1984; Pearson & Johnson, 1978) helps students to bridge what they know about a topic and what they learn from information in the text or from another information source. Semantic Mapping actively involves students in graphically organizing information in categorical form. The four-step strategy (brainstorming, categorizing, reading, and revising the categories) helps students to become active readers and, in the process, remember new vocabulary and information.

Procedure

1. Choose a major concept or topic being studied by the class. In elementary science, for example, the life cycle of the butterfly is a frequently-studied topic.

2. Draw an oval on the board, an overhead transparency, or use the reproducible master on page 109. Write *butterflies* in the center of the oval. Ask students to brainstorm words related to their study of *butterflies*. For example, words related to *butterflies* might be *chrysalis, caterpillar, wings, leaves, cocoon, branches, pouch, moths, colors, egg, eaten by birds, larva.* Try to keep the number of responses to ten or twelve for ease of management. List words related to the topic on the board or an overhead transparency.

3. When the brainstormed words have been listed, read them aloud and ask students to think of headings that the words might be clustered under. Students need to label their clusters or give them titles to indicate what the words have in common. Put cluster headings in the ovals surrounding the center oval. You may wish to have students complete this step in small cooperative groups. It is often possible for some of the brainstormed words to become category headings. For example, the labels for clusters related to the life cycle of butterflies might be *How They Look, How They Change, What They Eat,* and *Enemies.*

4. Next, have students try to put the brainstormed words on lines branching from the appropriate oval, showing connections to the idea within the oval. When you and the students have completed the classification and categorization of the words, invite students to share the labels for each of their clusters and the words they have included under each heading. You may wish to record these on the board or on an overhead transparency created from the reproducible master on page 109.

5. It is important that students share their reasons for their clustering decisions. This sharing stimulates students to think of the words in a variety of ways, consider their meanings, connect them, and see relationships among the words.

6. If used as a prereading activity, ask students to then read the text and evaluate their headings and the words they have clustered together. They may need to rename some of their headings and/or rearrange some words based on additional information in the lesson.

7. If used as a postreading activity, students may want to return to the text and confirm their reasons for and accuracy of their clusters and connected words.

8. The strategy work can be extended over the course of several days as students acquire additional information about the topic. More words can be added to the clusters as students expand their knowledge and increase the connections they make between and among the words. If desired, different colored inks can be used for words added from additional sources or at different times, thus graphically illustrating the expanding knowledge base of the students and the desirability of using a variety of resources in acquiring information.

9. When the semantic maps are complete, have students work individually or in pairs to write a summary of the information in one of the clusters or write a longer piece about the topic, using each one of the clusters of information as a paragraph in a main idea-detail piece. Students may also use their completed semantic maps as study aids.

References

Heimlich, J.E., & Pittelman, S.D. (1986). *Semantic mapping: Classroom applications.* Newark, DE: International Reading Association.

Johnson, D.D., & Pearson, P.D. (1984). *Teaching reading vocabulary.* New York: Holt, Rinehart & Winston.

Pearson, P.D., & Johnson, D.D. (1978). *Teaching reading comprehension.* New York: Holt, Rinehart & Winston.

Semantic Mapping

Life Cycle of Butterflies

(topic)

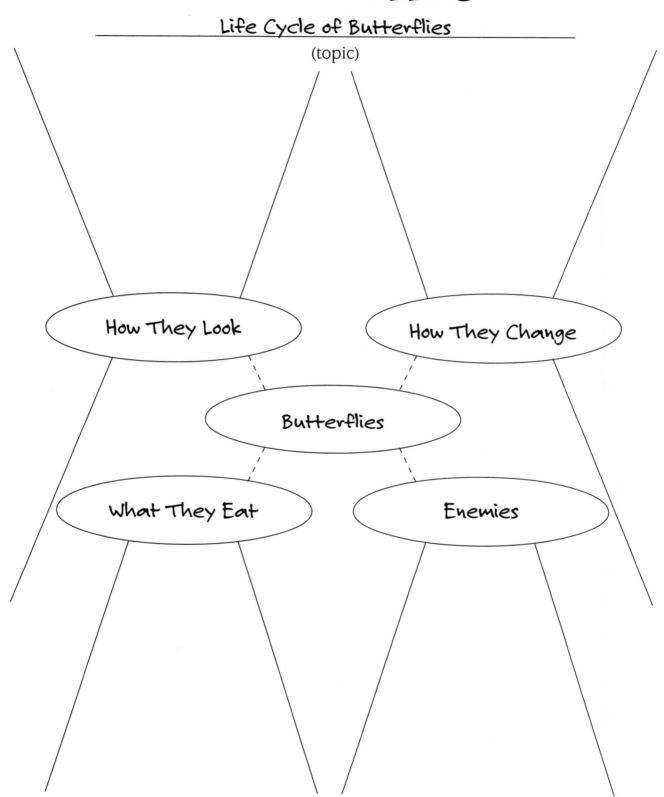

- How They Look
- How They Change
- Butterflies
- What They Eat
- Enemies

Name _____ Date _____

Semantic Mapping

_____
(topic)

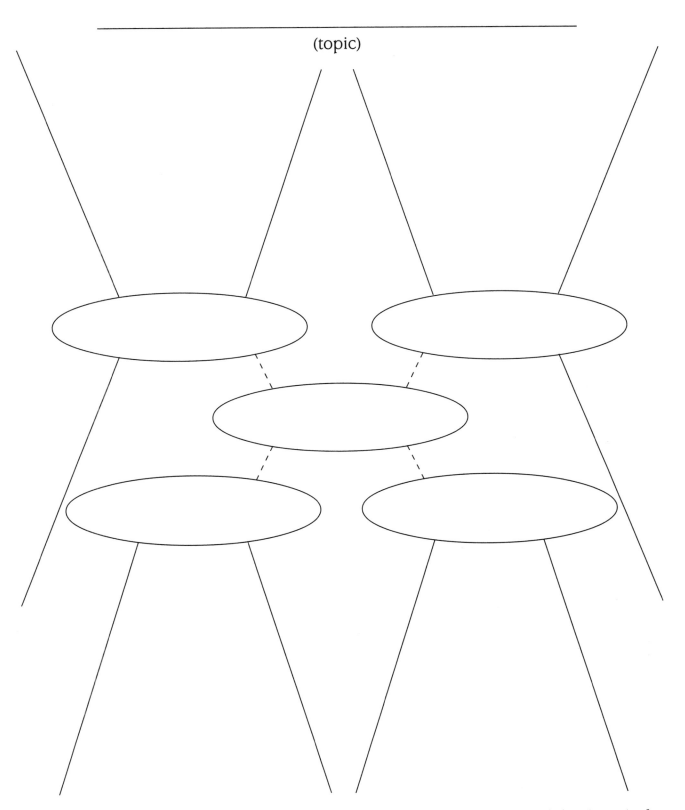

From Jerry L. Johns, Susan Davis Lenski, and Roberta L. Berglund, *Comprehension and Vocabulary Strategies for the Primary Grades*. Copyright © 2003 by Kendall/Hunt Publishing Company (1-800-247-3458, ext. 4 or 5). May be reproduced for noncommercial educational purposes within the guidelines noted on the copyright page.

 # SKETCH TO STRETCH

FOCUS		TEXT		WHEN			WHY									HOW			
Comprehension	Vocabulary	Narrative	Informational	Before Reading	During Reading	After Reading	Predicting	Connecting	Questioning	Using Text Structure	Visualizing	Inferring	Summarizing	Synthesizing	Determining Importance	Individual	Partner	Small Group	Whole Group
●		●	●			●		●			●	●					●	●	●

Description

Sketch to Stretch (Short, Harste, & Burke, 1996) is a strategy that offers students a way to extend meaning and respond to narrative text, informational text, or poetry following reading. Sketch to Stretch assists students in using visualization to support comprehension (McLaughlin & Allen, 2002). It also can be used as a means to help students become more comfortable in talking and working in pairs and in small groups. After students read or listen to a selection, they are asked to draw a sketch showing what the passage means to them. Sketch to Stretch can be introduced and modeled during class read-aloud experiences and can then be moved into small group settings to encourage rich discussions.

Procedure

1. Begin by reading a selected text aloud to students and modeling a think-aloud while doing so. For example, while reading aloud the informational book *Apes!* (Harrison, 1999), you might say the following.

    As I look at this book, I am thinking, I wonder what we might learn about apes. The drawing on the cover looks very real to me, so I think this book might give me information about apes. I don't think it is going to be a make-believe story. [Read the first page: They run and wrestle. They're very curious. And they love to play just like you! They're apes!]

    Hmmm, this sounds a lot like our recess time! Maybe apes are more like humans than I thought. As we read the rest of this book, I wonder if we are going to learn more about how apes are like us? The illustrator has drawn some pictures to help us understand more about apes, and I am going to be making some pictures in my mind as I read.

2. After finishing the read-aloud and think-aloud, introduce the idea of making a drawing of the ideas or feelings you have about the text. You might say the following.

I am going to do my best to sketch what I was thinking as I read. When I finish, I want you to guess what you think I was remembering and thinking about. I am not going to color my picture or make it ready to hang on the bulletin board in our artist's corner. I am just going to keep my sketch in my journal to help me remember something about the book, how I felt about it, or a connection I made with it.

3. After several students have had a chance to hypothesize about your interpretation of the text, you might say the following.

I drew a sketch of a gorilla with a happy expression holding a kitten because I remember learning about Koko the gorilla who had a pet kitten and actually named it! I will use this sketch to help me remember that apes have feelings and can communicate through expressions and sounds. My sketch also helps me think about whether it is right to keep apes in zoos behind bars. How would we like that? So my sketch shows me one idea I got from the book, a connection I made with something I already knew about, and it helps me remember how I felt when I read about the apes.

Remember, we don't need to be great artists or illustrators to sketch a picture after we read to help us remember what we read about or how it made us feel. Sketches like mine are another way we can make connections with our reading and learning. Each of us may read the same text, but our sketches may be very different. One isn't right and another one wrong. We all have different interests and backgrounds, so how we interpret the same texts may be quite different.

4. Give students an opportunity to draw sketches of their ideas about the *Apes!* book.

5. When students have finished their sketches, invite each person to show his or her sketch. Before the artist can say what the sketch is about, other students need to share their hypotheses about the sketch. Finally, it is the artist's turn to explain the sketch and how it helps the artist to connect with the text or with a feeling about it. (See Save the Last Word for the Artist on page 112.)

6. Continue sharing sketches until most students have shared or until students understand the procedures for Sketch to Stretch.

7. Explain to students that they will be using Sketch to Stretch in their small group or partner time and that they will need to remember to follow the ideas for Save the Last Word for the Artist (see page 112) when they get in their groups or work with a partner.

References

Harrison, C. (1999). *Apes!* New York: McClanahan.

McLaughlin, M., & Allen, M.B. (2002). *Guided comprehension: A teaching model for grades 3–8.* Newark, DE: International Reading Association.

Short, K.G., Harste, J.C., & Burke, C. (1996). *Creating classrooms for authors and inquirers* (2nd ed.). Portsmouth, NH: Heinemann.

Save the Last Word for the Artist

1. Choose someone to begin.

2. Have the first person show his or her sketch, but don't say anything about it.

3. Take turns. Have each person say something like this about the sketch.

   I think this sketch is about . . .

   I think the artist feels . . .

   I think the artist has made a connection with . . .

4. When each person has had a chance to say something about the sketch, it is the artist's turn to talk.

5. The artist should say something like this:

   My sketch is about . . .

   My sketch shows how I felt when . . .

   My sketch shows how I made a connection to . . .

6. The next member of the group should share his or her sketch.

7. Keep sharing sketches until everyone has had a turn.

8. Now, pick one sketch from your group to share with the class.

From Jerry L. Johns, Susan Davis Lenski, and Roberta L. Berglund, *Comprehension and Vocabulary Strategies for the Primary Grades*. Copyright © 2003 by Kendall/Hunt Publishing Company (1-800-247-3458, ext. 4 or 5). May be reproduced for noncommercial educational purposes within the guidelines noted on the copyright page.

STORY FACE

FOCUS		TEXT		WHEN			WHY									HOW			
Comprehension	Vocabulary	Narrative	Informational	Before Reading	During Reading	After Reading	Predicting	Connecting	Questioning	Using Text Structure	Visualizing	Inferring	Summarizing	Synthesizing	Determining Importance	Individual	Partner	Small Group	Whole Group
●		●				●				●	●				●	●		●	●

Description

Understanding the elements of narrative text structure is an important key to comprehending stories. The Story Face strategy (Staal, 2000) is an adaptation of story mapping. Students use the graphic organizer shaped like a face to assist them in visualizing, identifying, understanding, and remembering story elements. The eyes represent the setting and main characters. The eyelashes can be used for adding descriptions and secondary characters. The nose represents the problem and the mouth represents the story's events and solution. The Story Face is best used after students have had experience with more traditional story maps.

Procedure

1. Select a book that has clearly identified story elements. For example, the books in the Clifford series by Norman Bridwell usually have a limited number of main characters, a clear problem, and events that lead to a resolution of the problem.

2. Make an overhead transparency of the Story Face reproducible master on page 116 and duplicate copies for students.

3. Write the words, *setting, characters, problem, events,* and *solution* on an overhead transparency or on the board. Review the words with students and remind them of the meaning of the words. You could say the following.

> Today when I read to you, I would like you to think about the main parts of the story as you listen. Let's review the things that all stories have in common. First, there is a setting. The setting is where and when the story takes place. Stories also have characters. Characters can be animals or people. The characters are who the story is about. Stories also have a problem. The problem leads the characters to take some actions to solve it. What happens are the events of the story. The event that solves the problem is called the solution. Now that we have reviewed the main elements of a story, let's read!

4. Read the story, *Clifford Gets a Job* (Bridwell, 1965) to the students.

5. After reading the story to the group, complete the Story Face together as follows.

"Where did the story take place?" Students may respond, "In and around Clifford's home town." Write their responses in the circle labeled *Setting*. If students wish to add descriptive words about the setting, write them on the eyelashes above the *Setting* eye. Tell students that when you go to a place, you usually use your eyes to see what the setting looks like.

Next ask students, "Who were the main characters in the story?" As students answer "Clifford, Emily Elizabeth, and robbers," write the names of the characters in the circle labeled *Characters*. Use the eyelashes above the character's eye for additional descriptive words or the secondary characters, *farmer* and *police*. Tell students that when you go somewhere, your eyes help you see the characters.

Ask students to identify the problem in the story. Help them to identify that Clifford's food was costing too much money, and he was going to lose his home. He needed to find a job. Write the elements of the problem in the appropriate box representing the nose on the Story Face. Tell students that sometimes our noses cause problems, for example, when we get a cold or when we bump our nose when we are playing.

Next, ask students to identify the main events of the story. Write each event in one of the *Events* circles representing the Story Face mouth.

Clifford joined the circus, but he got in trouble.

Clifford worked on a farm, but he wrecked the barn.

Clifford caught some robbers.

Tell students, "Mouths help us know how people are feeling. Often the events that have happened in people's lives affect how they look, whether they are smiling or feeling sad."

Finally, ask students, "What was the solution to Clifford's problem?" When students offer that the police rewarded Clifford with dog food, write the solution in the appropriate circle.

6. To conclude the lesson, review the story elements one more time and remind students to think about the things all stories have in common. Remind them that knowing these elements will help them better understand stories when they are reading.

References

Bridwell, N. (1965). *Clifford gets a job*. New York: Scholastic.

Staal, L.A. (2000). The Story Face: An adaptation of story mapping that incorporates visualization and discovery learning to enhance reading and writing. *The Reading Teacher, 54*, 26–31.

Story Face

Clifford Gets a Job
Title

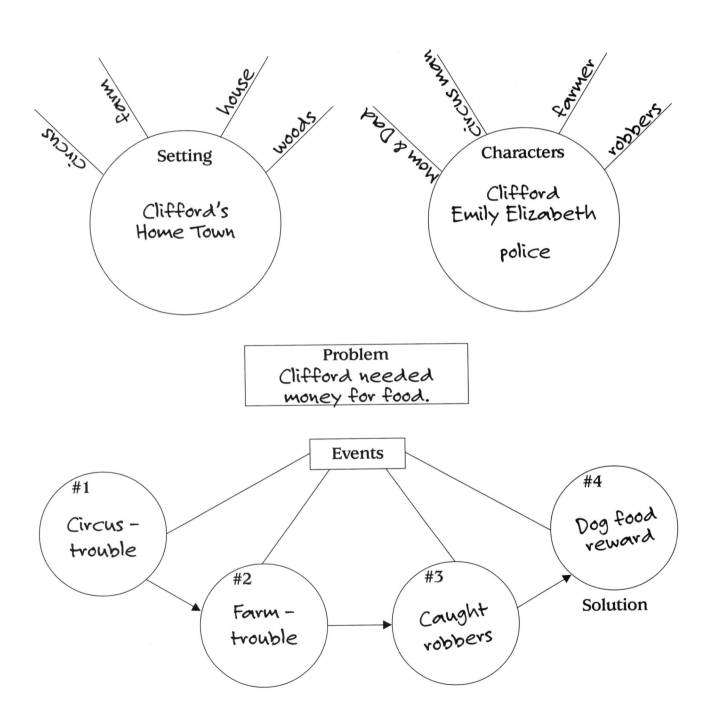

Setting

Clifford's Home Town

circus · barn · house · woods

Characters

Clifford
Emily Elizabeth

police

Mom & Dad · circus man · farmer · robbers

Problem
Clifford needed money for food.

Events

#1 Circus - trouble

#2 Farm - trouble

#3 Caught robbers

#4 Dog food reward

Solution

From Jerry L. Johns, Susan Davis Lenski, and Roberta L. Berglund, *Comprehension and Vocabulary Strategies for the Primary Grades*. Copyright © 2003 by Kendall/Hunt Publishing Company (1-800-247-3458, ext. 4 or 5). May be reproduced for noncommercial educational purposes within the guidelines noted on the copyright page.

Name _____ Date _____

Story Face

_____
Title

Setting

Characters

Problem

Events

#1

#2

#3

#4

Solution

Based on Staal, L.A. (2000). The Story Face: An adaptation of story mapping that incorporates visualization and discovery learning to enhance reading and writing. *The Reading Teacher*, *54*, 26–31.

From Jerry L. Johns, Susan Davis Lenski, and Roberta L. Berglund, *Comprehension and Vocabulary Strategies for the Primary Grades*. Copyright © 2003 by Kendall/Hunt Publishing Company (1-800-247-3458, ext. 4 or 5). May be reproduced for noncommercial educational purposes within the guidelines noted on the copyright page.

 # STORY PYRAMID

FOCUS		TEXT		WHEN			WHY									HOW			
Comprehension	Vocabulary	Narrative	Informational	Before Reading	During Reading	After Reading	Predicting	Connecting	Questioning	Using Text Structure	Visualizing	Inferring	Summarizing	Synthesizing	Determining Importance	Individual	Partner	Small Group	Whole Group
●		●				●		●						●	●	●	●	●	●

Description

The Story Pyramid (Waldo, 1991) is an instructional strategy to help students identify and summarize some of the major parts of a story. Like the Predict-O-Gram (see page 85), a Story Pyramid helps students learn the major features of narrative text.

Procedure

1. Select a story that has a clear plot outline. Read the story to students or have them read it independently.

2. Place a copy of the Story Pyramid on chart paper, the board, or an overhead transparency. Tell students that the Story Pyramid will be used to help identify some of the major parts of the story. You might say the following.

    > We have just read *Now One Foot, Now the Other* (de Paola, 1981). Notice that lines on the chart paper are in the shape of a pyramid. [Demonstrate by drawing a pyramid outside the lines with a marker.]

3. Draw students' attention to the word *character* under the top line. Explain that *character* refers to an important person or animal in the story. Invite a student to share a name and write it on the line.

4. Then move to the second line of the Story Pyramid and ask a volunteer to give two words that describe the *setting* or where and when the story takes place.

5. Use a similar approach with the remaining items of the Story Pyramid. After the Story Pyramid has been completed, spend some time discussing how this strategy can help students remember the story. You might also complete another Story Pyramid for the story if there are multiple characters and events. A sample Story Pyramid follows.

Story Pyramid

Now One Foot, Now the Other by T. de Paola

<u>   Bob   </u>

Character

<u> home </u>   <u> years </u>

Two words that describe the setting

<u> funny </u>   <u> kind </u>   <u> teacher </u>

Three words that describe the character

<u> Bob </u> <u> had </u> <u> a </u> <u> stroke. </u>

Four words to describe the problem

<u> Bobby </u> <u> taught </u> <u> Bob </u> <u> to </u> <u> walk. </u>

Five words that describe the solution

6. As students gain confidence with the Story Pyramid, divide the class into groups of three or four. Each group then identifies a character in the story, the setting, and some events in the story. The blank Story Pyramid that follows can be completed by each group independently. Then each group can share its Story Pyramid with the class.

References

de Paola, T. (1981). *Now one foot, now the other*. New York: G.P. Putnam's Sons.

Waldo, B. (1991). Story pyramid. In J.M. Macon, D. Bewell, & M. Vogt (Eds.), *Responses to literature: Grades K–8* (pp. 23–24). Newark, DE: International Reading Association.

 # Story Pyramid

DIRECTIONS Fill in the blanks below to make a Story Pyramid.

_____
Character

_____ _____
Two words that describe the setting

_____ _____ _____
Three words that describe the character

_____ _____ _____ _____
Four words to describe the problem

_____ _____ _____ _____
Five words that describe an event

_____ _____ _____ _____ _____ _____
Six words that describe the solution

From Jerry L. Johns, Susan Davis Lenski, and Roberta L. Berglund, *Comprehension and Vocabulary Strategies for the Primary Grades*. Copyright © 2003 by Kendall/Hunt Publishing Company (1-800-247-3458, ext. 4 or 5). May be reproduced for noncommercial educational purposes within the guidelines noted on the copyright page.

Name _____ Date _____

Story Pyramid

DIRECTIONS Fill in the blanks below to make a Story Pyramid.

_____
Character

_____ _____
Two words that describe the setting

_____ _____ _____
Three words that describe the character

_____ _____ _____ _____
Four words to describe the problem

_____ _____ _____ _____ _____
Five words that describe an event

_____ _____ _____ _____ _____ _____
Six words that describe the solution

_____ _____ _____ _____ _____ _____ _____
Seven words that describe why the story was written

From Jerry L. Johns, Susan Davis Lenski, and Roberta L. Berglund, *Comprehension and Vocabulary Strategies for the Primary Grades*. Copyright © 2003 by Kendall/Hunt Publishing Company (1-800-247-3458, ext. 4 or 5). May be reproduced for noncommercial educational purposes within the guidelines noted on the copyright page.

STRATEGY GLOVE

FOCUS		TEXT		WHEN			WHY									HOW			
Comprehension	Vocabulary	Narrative	Informational	Before Reading	During Reading	After Reading	Predicting	Connecting	Questioning	Using Text Structure	Visualizing	Inferring	Summarizing	Synthesizing	Determining Importance	Individual	Partner	Small Group	Whole Group
●		●	●		●	●			●	●					●	●	●	●	●

Description

This multisensory approach uses visual clues, combined with teacher questioning, to place pictures on actual gloves. The questions relate to the icons and help students learn the strategy so they can use it independently during reading (Newman, 2001/2002). The goal is to help students internalize questioning strategies so they can improve their understanding of text. There are three different gloves to help with predictions, narrative text, and informational text. The informational text structure glove is explained below. It can also be used with narrative text.

Procedure

1. Construct a strategy glove (see example on page 124). The materials needed include an inexpensive white or light colored glove, a small lock fastened in the palm of the glove, and keys fastened on each of the fingers. The lock signifies the main idea, and the keys are details that support the main idea. Newman (2001/2002) recommends using Velcro® to fasten the lock and keys on the glove. Glue the soft side of the Velcro® to the glove and attach the sticky side to the lock and keys that will be attached to the glove. Allow the glue to dry a day before attaching the items to the glove. Plastic storage bags can be used for the glove, lock, and keys.

2. Introduce the glove to students by saying the following or adapting it to suit your mode of presentation for the book you choose.

    > Take a look at what's on my hand. It's a special type of glove that can help you understand what you read. Some of the stories and books we read are informational. That means they give us facts about various topics. The lock on this glove represents the main topic and the keys represent the facts or details about the main topic or idea. As I read *Look at These Animals* (Christopher, 2003), I'm going to show you how the glove is used.

3. Show the cover of the book and invite students to predict what the book might be about. A sample class discussion follows.

Mr. Reed: What can you tell from the cover of the book?

Lacy: It's going to be about animals. I can see a dog and cat on the cover. The dog is just a puppy.

Mr. Reed: Are the animals in this book real or make believe?

Josh: They are probably going to be real because the pictures are of real animals.

Mr. Reed: You are correct. I'll read the first couple of pages and then we will use the Strategy Glove.

4. Read the text about the animals that are called mammals. Show the pictures and have students identify the dog, cat, guinea pig, hamster, and rabbit. Then ask a volunteer to share the special name for the animals (mammals) and some of the characteristics they possess. A sample discussion follows.

Mr. Reed: What is the scientific name we call these animals?

Sophia: They are mammals.

Mr. Reed: That's right. Look at my glove. I'm going to take the lock and attach it to the palm of the glove. The lock stands for mammals, the main idea or topic of these pages. Now look at the keys I'm holding. They stand for some of the facts or details I read about the mammals. Tell me some of those details, and I will put a key on a finger for each detail you mention.

Zach: Mammals can be big or small.

Mr. Reed: That's right. I will attach a key for that detail about mammals.

Lacy: Mammals have hair or fur on their bodies.

Cherith: And mammals make milk for their babies.

Mr. Reed: Very good! I'll add a key for the fur or hair and another key for the idea that mother mammals make milk for their babies.

5. Continue reading the book. The main idea or topic of the next two pages is "birds." The details are "covered with feathers," "have wings," and "mother birds lay eggs." Invite students to offer their ideas and add the lock and keys. Clarify and reinforce as necessary.

6. As you read about fish, amphibians, and reptiles, invite students to help you identify the main idea and details for each group. You may wish to have a student wear the glove and add the lock and keys as other students share information about a particular group of animals. See page 124 for a completed Strategy Glove for amphibians.

7. Continue using the Strategy Glove with a variety of texts. Students enjoy using the actual gloves, so you may want to make several. Once students have grasped the basic idea, you could use the reproducible master of the Strategy Glove on page 125.

8. The Strategy Glove can also be used for writing a paragraph using a main idea or topic and the details.

References

Christopher, G. (2003). *Look at these animals*. New York: Sadlier-Oxford.

Newman, G. (2001/2002). Comprehension strategy gloves. *The Reading Teacher, 55,* 329–332.

Strategy Glove for Informational Text

Look at These Animals by G. Christopher

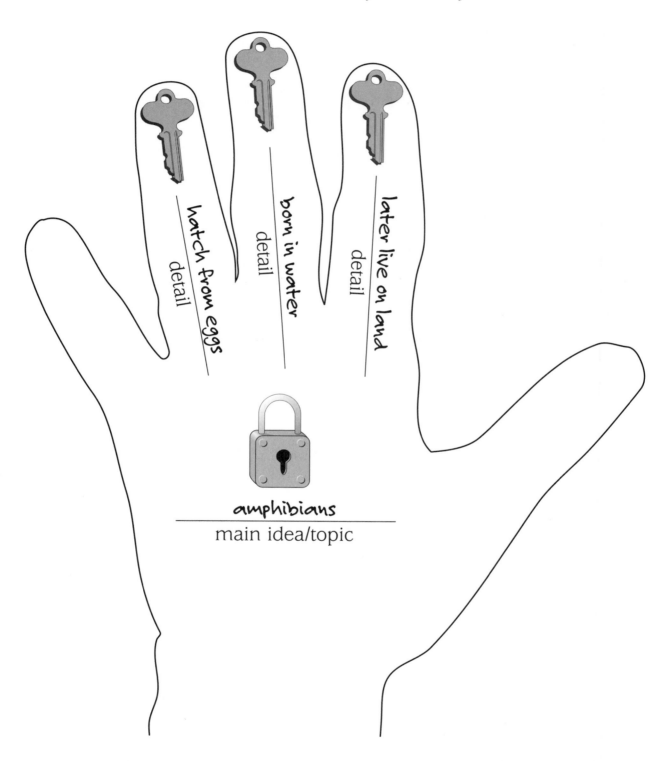

hatch from eggs
detail

born in water
detail

later live on land
detail

amphibians
main idea/topic

Name _____ Date _____

📖 **Strategy Glove**

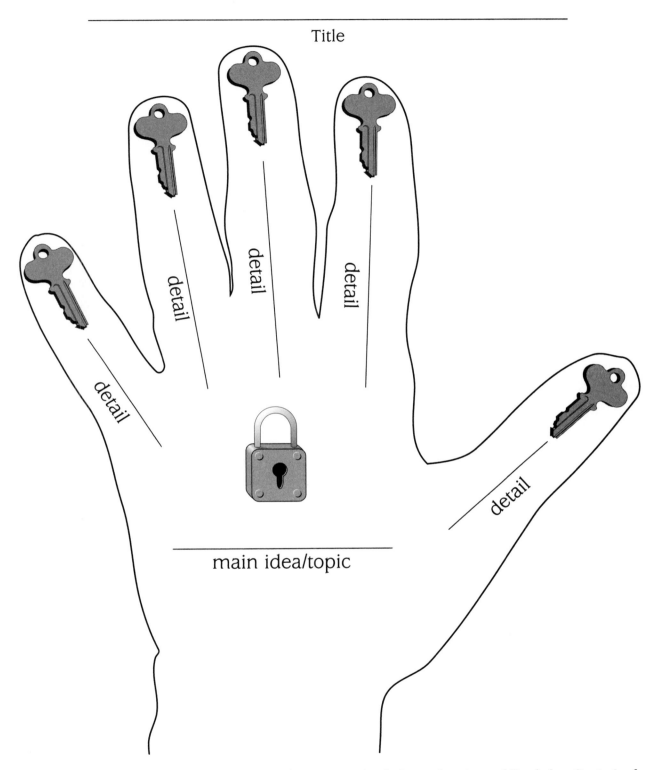

Title _____

detail

detail

detail

detail

detail

detail

main idea/topic _____

From Jerry L. Johns, Susan Davis Lenski, and Roberta L. Berglund, *Comprehension and Vocabulary Strategies for the Primary Grades*. Copyright © 2003 by Kendall/Hunt Publishing Company (1-800-247-3458, ext. 4 or 5). May be reproduced for noncommercial educational purposes within the guidelines noted on the copyright page.

TIERED BINGO

FOCUS		TEXT		WHEN			WHY									HOW			
Comprehension	Vocabulary	Narrative	Informational	Before Reading	During Reading	After Reading	Predicting	Connecting	Questioning	Using Text Structure	Visualizing	Inferring	Summarizing	Synthesizing	Determining Importance	Individual	Partner	Small Group	Whole Group
●	●	●	●	●	●	●	●	●	●	●	●	●	●	●	●	●			

Description

Students need opportunities to make choices about the reading and writing strategies that they use. Choice about activities provides students with an understanding that they can learn to become independent strategic readers. A strategy that promotes reading choices is Tiered Bingo (Tomlinson, 1999). Tiered Bingo has another benefit: you can differentiate the strategies that you ask students to use.

Procedure

1. Identify several reading and writing strategies and activities that you would like students to accomplish over a number of days. Prepare a range of activities from those that would challenge your best readers to those that could be completed independently by readers who struggle.

2. Duplicate the reproducible master of Tiered Bingo on page 130 and write the activities you have selected on the blanks. Vary the activities by level of difficulty.

3. Tell students that they will be using the Tiered Bingo sheet during independent work time for several days. Explain to students that they will be allowed to choose activities to accomplish. Say something like the following.

    > Today we're going to do something different in our classroom. You're going to get the chance to decide which activity you want to complete each day. If you are making your own decision, the student sitting next to you might be working on a different activity than you are, so don't let that surprise you.

    > It will be something like when you're getting ready to play soccer. Before the game, some of you practice kicking the ball, some of you practice shooting, and some of you practice passing the ball to a friend. Your team is doing several different things at once. That's what will happen when our class does Tiered Bingo.

4. Review with students how to play Bingo. You might use a Bingo sheet with numbers or letters so that students can practice playing. Decide whether you want to award prizes or points for students who make a Bingo or whether you want students to complete a certain number of squares. If you have developed activities with a range of difficulties, however, you should not ask students to complete the entire Tiered Bingo sheet.

5. Explain what each of the activities in the squares means. You might use icons or pictures for some activities so students can use the strategies independently.

6. A sample Tiered Bingo sheet using reading and writing activities, one with reading strategies, and a reproducible master of Tiered Bingo follows on pages 128–130.

Reference

Tomlinson, C.A. (1999). *The differentiated classroom: Responding to the needs of all learners.* Alexandria, VA: Association for Supervision and Curriculum Development.

📖 Tiered Bingo

Read an ABC book.	Write a letter to a friend.	Read the room.
Use magnetic letters to make 10 new words.	Read a book from your basket.	Listen to a story on tape.
Write the first and last names of 6 students.	Write the capital and small letters of the alphabet.	Write a story about your family.

From Jerry L. Johns, Susan Davis Lenski, and Roberta L. Berglund, *Comprehension and Vocabulary Strategies for the Primary Grades*. Copyright © 2003 by Kendall/Hunt Publishing Company (1-800-247-3458, ext. 4 or 5). May be reproduced for noncommercial educational purposes within the guidelines noted on the copyright page.

📖 Tiered Bingo

Make a prediction while reading.	Make connections using Brain Surfing.	Find some new vocabulary words as you read.
After reading, sketch how the book made you feel.	Use DR-TA while reading.	Make a Story Face.
Question the Author while reading.	Create a Story Pyramid.	Fill out Four Square on a new word.

From Jerry L. Johns, Susan Davis Lenski, and Roberta L. Berglund, *Comprehension and Vocabulary Strategies for the Primary Grades*. Copyright © 2003 by Kendall/Hunt Publishing Company (1-800-247-3458, ext. 4 or 5). May be reproduced for noncommercial educational purposes within the guidelines noted on the copyright page.

Tiered Bingo

From Jerry L. Johns, Susan Davis Lenski, and Roberta L. Berglund, *Comprehension and Vocabulary Strategies for the Primary Grades*. Copyright © 2003 by Kendall/Hunt Publishing Company (1-800-247-3458, ext. 4 or 5). May be reproduced for noncommercial educational purposes within the guidelines noted on the copyright page.

 # VOCABULARY ANCHORS

FOCUS		TEXT		WHEN			WHY									HOW			
Comprehension	Vocabulary	Narrative	Informational	Before Reading	During Reading	After Reading	Predicting	Connecting	Questioning	Using Text Structure	Visualizing	Inferring	Summarizing	Synthesizing	Determining Importance	Individual	Partner	Small Group	Whole Group
	●		●	●			●	●										●	●

Description

Vocabulary Anchors (Winters, 2001) provide a visual organizer to assist students in actively exploring, connecting with, and using content vocabulary. Vocabulary Anchors are best used to introduce new terms that are not highly complex or abstract and for which students may have strong prior conceptual knowledge and association. Vocabulary Anchors provide a student-friendly means of helping students access and use their background knowledge to build connections from the known to the new.

Procedure

1. Display a drawing or picture of a boat that appears to be floating on water. You may want to introduce the concept of Vocabulary Anchors using the example below.

   Most of you have seen boats floating on lakes or rivers near where we live or perhaps when you were on vacation. Many of you may have experience being in a boat when it was floating. When boats are near the dock, they are usually tied to a post or raised out of the water to keep them from floating away. Sometimes when we are out in boats, far away from the dock, we want to stay in one place for awhile and there is nothing near us to tie the boat to. Does anyone know how you keep a boat in one spot and keep it from drifting when you are floating out in a river or lake? [Elicit from students that an anchor is one means of keeping a boat from drifting.] Does anyone know how the anchor is connected to the boat? [Elicit from the students that the anchor is attached to the boat with a chain, rope, or strong line called a tethering line.]

2. Explain that when we are learning something new, it helps to have something to connect our new ideas to. Connecting helps to keep them from drifting away, just like an anchor holds a boat in one place and keeps it from drifting away.

3. Present the boat and anchor graphic organizer (see page 134) and say the following.

> An anchor connected to the boat helps it stay in one place and keeps it from drifting away. We can use our experience with anchors to help us develop a way to remember new words or ideas in our reading and keep them from drifting away from us. We are going to call this drawing a Vocabulary Anchor. We can use Vocabulary Anchors to help us connect things we already know with things we are learning. This will help us remember them.

4. Present an example on an overhead transparency and model your thinking process for students as you complete the graphic organizer. For example, draw a boat or make a transparency of the graphic organizer on page 135 and write the term *orangutan* within the bottom of the boat. Then write a word that is similar to *orangutan* that students are likely to know inside the anchor beneath the boat, for example, *chimpanzee*. Tell students that this is an anchor word that helps you know something about the new boat word. Connect the two with a line to show that the anchor is connected to the boat. You might say the following.

> We are going to be learning about a kind of ape called an *orangutan*. We are going to call our new word our boat word. Here is a word I already know that might be something like our boat word. It's *chimpanzee*. I'm going to call that word our anchor word. *Orangutans* and *chimpanzees* are similar in that they both are *apes*. They are also *warm-blooded* and they can use their *thumbs* to grasp things, just like we do. I am going to write the words that help me know that *orangutans* and *chimpanzees* are similar right next to the tethering line connecting our anchor to our boat. I am going to put a plus (+) next to those words.

5. Write the words *apes, warm-blooded,* and *thumbs* adjacent to the tethering line and place a plus (+) before each word (see example on page 134).

6. Now describe how the two terms are different. As you describe these critical differences, write the words away from the boat and anchor, allowing them to float away from them. Put a minus (–) next to these words. You might say the following.

> Our boat word and our anchor word are not exactly alike. Let me tell you some ways that they are different. Orangutans live in Asia, while chimpanzees live in Africa. Also, orangutans are slow-moving and they live alone, while chimpanzees can move quickly and prefer to live in large groups of fifty or more. Because these words help us know how the terms *orangutan* and *chimpanzee* are different, I am going to write them like they are floating out away from our boat and anchor. I am going to put a minus (–) next to these words.

7. Write the words *Asia, slow-moving,* and *alone* in the space near the right side of the boat. Put a minus (–) in front of these words.

8. Turn your attention to the sail on the boat and ask the following question.

> What words might we write on the sail of our boat to help us remember our new boat word, *orangutan*? Words that we choose may be different for each of us, based on the experiences we have had. We all use our experiences to help us remember new words and ideas.

9. Ask one or more students to suggest words to put on the sail, explaining how these words will help them remember the new word. To model, you might share some words that you would use and explain why you chose them, perhaps sharing a memorable experience that helps you connect with the word. You might also draw a picture instead of, or in addition to, one or more of the words added to the sail.

> I remember going to the zoo with my nieces and we saw an orangutan. In fact, we saw a mother orangutan with a baby. She was holding it very close to her and swinging on a vine through the trees. Because of my memory, I am going to write *baby* and *vine* on my sail to help me remember the mother orangutan that I saw. Perhaps one of you could help me add pictures to my words by drawing a baby ape and a vine. When I look at my Vocabulary Anchor, I have lots of ways of remembering about *orangutans*. When I read more about apes, I might be able to add some more ideas to my boat picture.

10. Finally, review the Vocabulary Anchor with students and explain how students can use it to help them learn and remember a new term.

> Let's look at our boat again. The new word we want to learn and remember is written on our boat. It's our *boat word*. The anchor is a word that we already know that is something like our new word. It helps us connect what we already know to our new word. The words near the tethering line help us know how these two words are alike. The words floating out in the water away from the boat help us know how our *boat word* and our *anchor word* are different. Each of us can add words or pictures to the sail, based on things we already know, to help us remember our new *boat word* in our own special way.

11. As students become more familiar with the use of Vocabulary Anchors, you might provide them with partially-completed Vocabulary Anchors for some of the key vocabulary words in a specific chapter or unit. Students may also enjoy selecting words that should be *boat words* for a specific unit of study. This strategy can also be linked to Finding My Own Words on page 43.

Reference

Winters, R. (2001). Vocabulary anchors: Building conceptual connections with young readers. *The Reading Teacher, 54,* 659–662.

Vocabulary Anchors

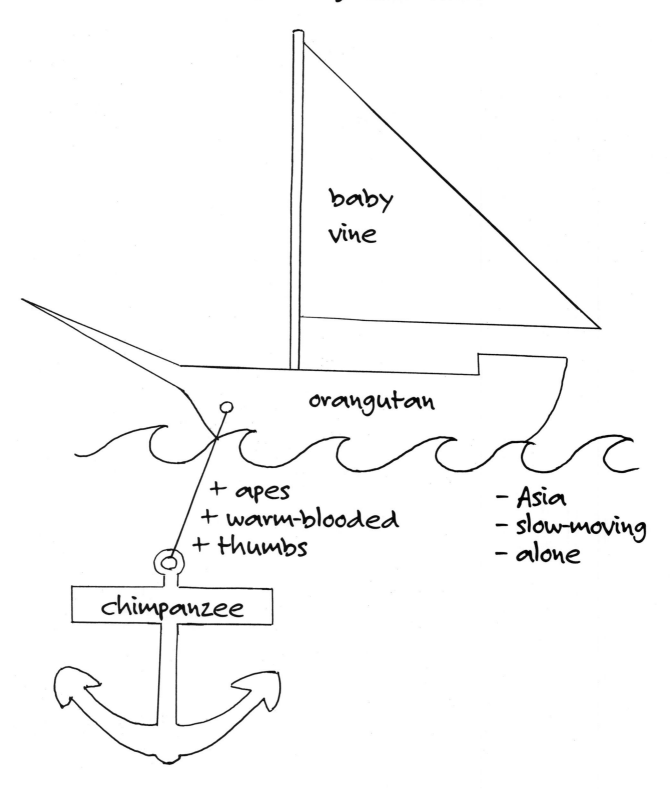

Name _____ Date _____

📖 **Vocabulary Anchors**

Based on Winters, R. (2001). Vocabulary anchors: Building conceptual connections with young readers. *The Reading Teacher, 54*, 659–662.

From Jerry L. Johns, Susan Davis Lenski, and Roberta L. Berglund, *Comprehension and Vocabulary Strategies for the Primary Grades.* Copyright © 2003 by Kendall/Hunt Publishing Company (1-800-247-3458, ext. 4 or 5). May be reproduced for noncommercial educational purposes within the guidelines noted on the copyright page.

WORD SORTS

FOCUS		TEXT		WHEN			WHY									HOW			
Comprehension	Vocabulary	Narrative	Informational	Before Reading	During Reading	After Reading	Predicting	Connecting	Questioning	Using Text Structure	Visualizing	Inferring	Summarizing	Synthesizing	Determining Importance	Individual	Partner	Small Group	Whole Group
●			●			●	●			●						●	●	●	●

Description

When students read narrative text, they automatically try to make sense of the story by identifying the characters, setting, plot, and theme. They also need to be proficient at identifying the patterns of informational texts (Yopp & Yopp, 2000). Most informational texts are organized by a combination of five patterns: main idea/detail, sequence, cause/effect, problem/solution, and comparison/contrast. It's not necessary for young readers to be able to tell you which text pattern they are reading, but it does increase the chances for rich comprehension if students can follow the logic of the text by understanding the way the thoughts are organized. A Word Sort is a strategy that can introduce students to the variety of patterns writers use when they write informational text.

Procedure

1. Remind students that stories are organized by a story grammar: plot, setting, characters, and theme. Review the terms if necessary.

2. Tell students that readers use their knowledge of text organization when they read. For example, you might say the following.

   > Yesterday, I read the book *Olivia* (Falconer, 2000) to you. As we read the book, you made lots of predictions about what Olivia would do. We followed Olivia through her day, and you even predicted that the book would end with Olivia going to bed. The story followed the same pattern as lots of other stories we have read.

3. Explain to students that some books they read will not be stories but will contain information. For example, you could say the following.

   > We also read another kind of story yesterday, a book about pigs on the farm. That book was not a made up story. It gave us information about pigs. Remember how we compared the book *Olivia* to the book about pigs?

4. Guide students to understand how narrative stories differ from informational text. An example of a classroom discussion follows.

Mr. Starkey: How were the books *Olivia* and the book about pigs different?

Jane: *Olivia* was a made-up story and the pig book wasn't.

Mr. Starkey: How else were they different?

Adam: *Olivia* didn't have any facts to learn.

Mr. Starkey: Any other differences?

Sheila: The pictures in the pig book were real.

5. Select an informational book to use to teach students text organization. Some books that seem to be informational books, such as *A Picture Book of Christopher Columbus* (Adler, 1991), are really narratives because they tell a story. Look for books that are not a story but that *explain* things.

6. Once you have selected an informational book, identify the text's organizational pattern. Most books written for young children will be written in the main idea/detail pattern.

7. Identify the main idea of a page or paragraph from the text. For example, you could use the section on Columbus's ships from the *Atlas of Exploration* for this activity. The main idea from that section is "Columbus took three ships on his journey west."

8. Make the Word Sort cards. On one of the cards, write the key words from the main idea sentence: Three ships. Then identify details from the paragraph and write them one per card. Examples could include Nina, Pinta, Santa Maria, tall-sided, three masts, large sails, and Columbus. A sample set of Word Sort cards can be found on page 138.

9. Read the selection to students or have students read independently. Tell students to look for the ways the text is organized.

10. Duplicate the word cards, cut them apart, and distribute them to students. Instruct students to arrange the cards in the order of the paragraph. Students should begin with the card "Three ships." Reinforce the idea that the first card is the main idea of the entire paragraph.

11. Provide students with many demonstrations and examples, emphasizing that informational texts are organized differently from fictional texts and use Word Sorts to illustrate how texts are organized.

12. A Word Sort reproducible master can be found on page 139.

References

Adler, D. (1991). *A picture book of Christopher Columbus*. New York: Scholastic.

Falconer, I. (2000). *Olivia*. New York: Atheneum.

Starkey, D. (1993). *Atlas of exploration*. New York: Scholastic.

Yopp, R.H., & Yopp, H.K. (2000). Sharing informational text with young children. *The Reading Teacher, 53,* 410–419.

Word Sort Cards

Atlas of Exploration by D. Starkey

Three ships	Nina
Tall sides	Large sails
Three masts	Pinta
Columbus	Santa Maria

Name _____   Date _____

 **Word Sort Cards**

_____

Title and Author

From Jerry L. Johns, Susan Davis Lenski, and Roberta L. Berglund, *Comprehension and Vocabulary Strategies for the Primary Grades*. Copyright © 2003 by Kendall/Hunt Publishing Company (1-800-247-3458, ext. 4 or 5). May be reproduced for noncommercial educational purposes within the guidelines noted on the copyright page.

 # NOTES/FAVORITE STRATEGIES

INDEX

 # NOTES/FAVORITE STRATEGIES

 # NOTES/FAVORITE STRATEGIES

 # NOTES/FAVORITE STRATEGIES